*Totterdown Lock and the entrance to the Feeder Canal are bottom right. St Mary Redcliffe's spire and the great sugar cone in its shadow are central.*

# BRISTOL
## PAST

*Donald Jones*

Phillimore

2000

Published by
PHILLIMORE & CO. LTD.
Shopwyke Manor Barn, Chichester, West Sussex

ISBN 1 86077 138 6

Printed and bound in Great Britain by
BIDDLES LTD.
Guildford, Surrey

*To Jeanne and Alysun*
*who were born in Bristol*
*and to Chris who grew up here.*

# Contents

# List of Illustrations

*Endpapers:* Lavar's panoramic view of Bristol, 1887

# *Illustration Acknowledgements*

The author would like to thank the following institutions and individuals who supplied or loaned photographs and illustrations and gave permission for their publication in this book:

BAE Systems, Airbus, 136, 137; Bristol Central Reference Library, 4, 5, 21, 32, 33, 95, 98, 101, 103, 105-7; Peter Harris and the Bristol Historical Association, 1, 2, 10, 11, 42, 43; Bristol Museums and Art Gallery, 29, 40, 41, 50, 51, 58, 69, 76, 77, 79, 90, 92, 93, 108, 109, endpapers and dustjacket illustration; Bristol Port Company, 132; Bristol Record Office, 14, 34, 38, 86, 104, 117, 158; John Cleverdon, 78; The Peter Davey Photograph Collection, 99, 100, 128, 146, 147; the late Nicholas Flatt, 16, 24, 35; John Harvey and Sons, 141; Don Loader, 'Memories', Corn Exchange, Bristol, 13, 15, 17, 19, 22, 25, 28, 46, 47, 57, 59-61, 64, 71, 75, 82, 87, 112-14, 119-21, 123-7, 129-131, 133, 134, 138, 139, 144, 145, 151-3, 155; Molly and George Luton, 70, 80, 94, 110, 118; Bruce Perrott, 122; Peter Ruck, 31, 52; The Michael J. Tozer Collection, 135; United Press Ltd., 148-150, 156; Robert Willis, 37.

Illustrations from G.F. Stone, *Bristol: As It Was—And As It Is* (1909); Francis B. Bickley (ed.), *The Little Red Book of Bristol*, Vol.1 (1900 edition), p.215; *Official Guide to the City of Bristol* (1913), p.96.

Maps: Ricart (1479); William Smith (1568); Jacob Millerd (1673); Michael Farr, map from E.J. Farr, A.T.G. Bower and R.M. Parsons, *Bristol City Docks Remembered, 1900-1973* (1986).

# *Introduction*

MANY HISTORIANS have written about particular aspects or periods of Bristol's past, but far fewer have attempted an overall view from Saxon origins to the present day. This may be because such a task inevitably involves generalisations which result in neutered and disinfected accounts doing nobody much good. This book takes a fresh look in the light of recent research. It has become possible to take a more balanced look at Bristol's involvement in the slave trade. We now know more about Victorian squalor as well as Cliftonian splendour; about Hotwells undertakers as well as courageous merchant venturers; and about Bristol's mobs as well as its aircraft manufacturers.

The author's intention is also to interest the reader in what has survived of Bristol's past despite the six major air raids of the Second World War which destroyed much of the old centre. Survival does not guarantee future preservation however. The story of what happened to Bristol's High Cross through neglect is typical and is a warning to all who love this city. Hitler was not responsible for road widening schemes through Redcliffe, destroying Canynge's House and Watt's Shot Tower. Nor did he drive a thoroughfare through Queen Square, not devise schemes putting dustbins and cars around 13th-century Quakers Friars. He did not propose 15-screen cinemas in our harbour development.

Bristol's origins were as a place of trade and commerce. The city docks, quays, man-made waterways, shipyards and hydraulic systems remain as a substantial legacy from the past and are exceptionally photogenic. The price of historical preservation is, as with so much else, eternal vigilance.

# Brigg-Stow, the Place of the Bridge

A VISITOR TO BRISTOL 1,000 years ago would have seen a bridge across the Avon, perhaps close to, but not at the exact spot of the present Bristol Bridge. The bridge permitted entrance into a defensible Anglo-Saxon settlement of less than 5,000 people living on the higher ground between the Frome and the Avon. The revival of raids of the Northmen in the early years of the reign of Ethelred the Unready would have made some sort of fortification necessary for a place which, as its coins show, already had a mint and was of considerable importance.

Bristol was not at first a fortified place. Recent archaeological evidence has shown that houses were demolished to clear space for a castle and that under the eastern rampart were Saxon foundations. During the excavations of 1962-3 at St Mary-le-Port, west of the castle, remains of a late Saxon street were found, with indications of iron working and leather working on the north side. The town was sited on a defensible position on three low hills rising fifty feet above the marshes. It provided safe anchorage seven miles up the Bristol Avon with access from the Severn Estuary and the Irish Sea. This facilitated trade with South Wales, North Somerset and Ireland.

The second hill, west of the Frome, was later chosen as the site of a monastery in 1140, but there may well have been an earlier Saxon church on the site. Legend tells of the burial of St Jordan there as well as of a visit by St Augustine. The third hill to the south of the original settlement became the centre of the Redcliffe development. Cut off from much of the rest of the country by the great forests of Kingswood and Horwood north of the river, and by the forest of Bedminster south of the river, Bristol developed through the only way open to it, the sea. From the second greatest tidal rise and fall in the world (37 feet under the Suspension Bridge, and 41 feet where the Avon joins the Severn) twice every 24 hours, millions of tons of water push up the gorge. Our visitor of 1,000 years ago would have seen many ships engaged in trade with Dublin, and the north Somerset and Devon coastline.

So significant had the port of Bristol become by the time the anonymous Domesday commissioners arrived in 1086 that it was recorded as paying 110 marks of silver to the king, a higher sum than that paid by any other town except London, York, Lincoln and Norwich. In addition to that sum the burgesses paid annually another 33 marks of silver and one of gold to Bishop Geoffrey of Coutances who was the

**1  Coins of Aethelred II (978-1016)**
*In 1000 there were mints at Bath, Gloucester, Axbridge and Malmesbury. These coins are evidence that Bristol also had a mint, and they are stamped by the moneyer Aelfward on Bric. They have survived at Stockholm, probably as Danegeld.*

**2    Quatrefoil Silver Penny of Cnut (1016–35)**
*This silver penny, struck by Aegelwine the moneyer at 'Bric', is to be seen at the Ashmolean, Oxford. Similar coins, struck at Dublin in 995, were modelled on pennies struck at Bath. The Bristol-Irish trade was probably a factor in the establishment of a Bristol mint.*

in Alfred's scheme for the defence of Wessex against the Danes Bristol is not listed among the important boroughs. The earliest reference in the Chronicle reveals Bristol as a significant port and point of departure to Dublin in 1051.

> And Earl Harold and Leofwine went to Bristol to the ship which Sweyn had equipped and provisioned for himself. And the king sent bishop Aldred from London with a force and they were to intercept him before he got on board, but they could not—or would not.

The town of Dublin developed in the late ninth and 10th centuries mainly, if not entirely, from Viking settlements. A Kildare coin hoard found in 1923, hidden around 991, comprised coins of which one-sixth came from west-country mints. Part of Bristol's pre-Conquest trade with Ireland was in white slaves.

effective viceroy for William I at Bristol. To coin such sums mints were necessary. In Saxon times mints were quite numerous. There were 75 in England in the reign of Aethelred II. Three coins with the words AELFWERD ON BRIC, probably minted at Bristol (978-1016), exist at Stockholm and in Copenhagen. By the time of Cnut (1016-1035), there were several moneyers in Bristol, including AELFWINE, AEGELWINE and LEOFWINE. Coins from Edward the Confessor's reign and from that of Harold I are not uncommon, but those for Harold II (January–October 1066) are very rare although one was found in the excavations at St Mary-le-Port in 1962.

The importance of Bristol in the late Anglo-Saxon period is shown in the Anglo-Saxon Chronicles, both before 1066, by its use as a base for Harold's ships in attacking Wales, and after Hastings, in 1067, by the unsuccessful attempt of Harold's sons to attack the town with a fleet.

> Harold's sons came from Ireland with a ship-force into the mouth of the Avon unexpectedly, and soon ravaged over all the area. They went to Bristol, and meant to break into the town, but the town-dwellers fought against them hardily; when they could win nothing from that town, they went to ship with what they had plundered, so fared to Somerset, and went inland there.

The passage in the Anglo-Saxon Chronicle for 1067 uses the word 'burh' when referring to Bristol, but

**3    The Harrowing of Hell relief in Bristol Cathedral, c.1050**
*The most dramatic evidence of the pre-Conquest church in the city, this is seven feet high and was discovered under the Chapter House floor. It had been used as a coffin lid, but the broadest part is at the feet and it was meant to be placed over a doorway.*

According to William of Malmesbury, writing in the 12th century in his *Life of Wulfstan*, 'One could see and lament over the ranks of the poor wretches roped together, young people of both sexes … they were daily exposed publicly for sale'. Through the preaching of Bishop Wulfstan of Worcester this traffic in human beings was stopped. It took him some time to swing opinion to his view, and he stayed in Bristol for two or three months at a time. He needed the support of Archbishop Lanfranc to persuade King William I to do without the duty paid on each slave. Even sixty years later Henry II found many slaves in Ireland, brought by Bristol traders who could still buy children from their parents in the market place.

Bristol's origins are Saxon. There was no Roman Bristol since, by the end of the first century, the region already contained two tribal capitals, Cirencester and Caerwent, one legionary fortress, Caerleon, one military colony for retired legionaries, Gloucester, and a spa town, Bath. There was a Roman naval support base and small fort at Sea Mills, and several villas in the area at Keynsham, Brislington, and Kingsweston, founded at the close of the third century, but no town. The tribesmen of the Dobunni, who lived in the Bristol area at the time of the Roman conquest, defended themselves behind ramparts on Blaise Castle Hill, Stokeleigh, and Clifton Down camp. There may have been farming communities at Ashton Park and along the Failand Ridge. Roman troops were withdrawn from the province between AD 383 and 407, and a particularly virulent plague decimated the population in this area in 443 AD. When the Anglo-Saxon Chronicle entry for 557 recorded that 'In this year Cuthwine and Ceawlin fought against the Britons … and they captured three cities, Gloucester, Cirencester and Bath', it may be that the Saxons captured little more than deserted ruins. Thus, archaeology has revealed that by the year 1000 a small fortified town, mint, market, and port had developed at the place of the bridge. It had good anchorage for ships and its

**4  A curtain wall tower of Bristol Castle, c.1914**
*This was at the rear of 41 Castle Street and was demolished in the 1930s to permit rebuilding. The 11 acres of the castle precincts extended to Halford's Gate (or Lord's Gate), now Lawford's Gate.*

inhabitants were involved in overseas trade, particularly with Ireland.

Domesday Book reveals how important Bristol had become as a trading centre, but it does not mention the existence of any castle. Yet Bishop Geoffrey's castle pre-dates 1088, and the excavations of 1949 revealed the foundations of such a building at the point where it could best dominate the trading town. After the final attack by Harold's sons in 1067 a royal stronghold had become a necessity. Under Bishop Geoffrey of Coutances, half-brother of William the Conqueror, and Roger de Mowbray his kinsman, Bristol became a centre for the party in

**5** *(left)*    ***Remains of Bristol Castle, c.1914***
*This shows a 13th-century vaulted chamber, which may have been the ante-chamber to the Great Hall. The Hall was exceptionally large, 108 ft. by 54 ft., and was built by Henry III.*

**6** *(below)*    ***St James' Priory***
*The priory was founded by Robert of Caen, Earl of Gloucester, c.1120. The nave has survived since 1374 as a parish church. There is a still unaltered clerestory of simple round-headed windows. Earl Robert was buried in 1148 somewhere in the choir.*

**7** *(opposite)*    ***Norman Gateway into Abbey of St Augustine's***
*Built c.1160, the four concentric courses of mouldings show complex decoration, chevron, lozenge, nail-head and chain. Robert Fitzharding, the future Lord Berkeley, was a prominent local townsman, much in favour with Robert of Gloucester, from whom he bought the site.*

England, dominating the east of the town. Robert also founded the Benedictine Priory of St James, dependent on Tewkesbury. The nave of the Priory still stands today at the Horsefair as it was made a parish church after 1374. The west front with its 'wheel' window and interlaced arcading is an important example of Romanesque architecture.

During the period of Stephen's reign, Robert of Gloucester and his half-sister, the Empress Matilda, effectively made Bristol the second capital of England. In 1141 King Stephen himself was imprisoned in the castle, following the Battle of Lincoln, but after nine months was exchanged by the Empress for Earl Robert. During this period Bristol made promising trade connections with Aquitaine and the other French possessions of the House of Anjou. The future Henry II spent part of his childhood in Bristol. Our detailed knowledge of this time derives from the writings of William of Malmesbury and Robert of Lewes, Bishop of Bath (1136-66), who was the probable author of *Gesta Stephani*.

Bristol's leading citizen at this time was a close adherent of the Gloucesters, Robert Fitzharding. He chose this moment to found Bristol's greatest religious house. One of his manors was Billeswick, which he had bought from Robert of Gloucester. In 1140, on a sloping tract of ground outside the town rising towards Brandon Hill, Fitzharding founded the community of Augustinian canons, the Abbey of St Augustine of Hippo. By the grant of Berkeley lands, forfeited from an adherent of King Stephen, Fitzharding became Lord of Berkeley and was able to endow the Abbey with lands. The glorious Chapter House remains his chief monument.

Another significant person in Bristol at this time was Lewin, son of Aelric. He was chamberlain of the Earl of Gloucester's household, and a tenant of lands both from the Earl of Gloucester and Fitzharding, in Bristol, Bedminster, Redcliffe, Keynsham and Dundry. It seems he gave his name to Lewin's Mead,

opposition to William Rufus. Their rising failed, and William Rufus installed Robert Fitzhamon, founder of Cardiff Castle and refounder of Tewkesbury Abbey, as his viceroy in this part of his kingdom. Fitzhamon staunchly supported the Conqueror's younger sons against Duke Robert of Normandy, their elder but easy-going brother, for nearly twenty years. However, he fell, mortally wounded, at Tenchbrai. Finally Duke Robert was captured by Henry I, his brother, and imprisoned for 28 years at Bristol Castle and at Cardiff.

Fitzhamon left four daughters, one of whom was married abroad. Two were made Abbesses and effectively sidelined. Mabel, the eldest daughter, married King Henry's bastard son by a Welsh lady called Nesta. He was Robert, Earl of Gloucester, and he rebuilt Bristol Castle, *c*.1120-30, as a great rectangular stone keep, as at London. William Wyrecestre says it was 110 feet by 95 feet in exterior dimensions, and it was among the strongest in

*8 (left)* **Chapter House, Abbey of St Augustine's, built c.1150**
*This extraordinarily rich room was reduced in size by the Riots of 1831, the rioters smashing up one end. It is still the finest Norman Chapter House in the country. William Wyrecester gives the original dimensions as 71 ft. by 25 ft. The arcaded recesses were used as seats by the monks.*

*9 (below)* **St Mary Redcliffe, Inner North Porch, built c.1180**
*This seems to have been the focal point around which the church was rebuilt in 1280. It is part of the original 12th-century church which stood on the site where the shrine of Our Lady stood. From 1280 Simon de Burton, six times Mayor of Bristol, contributed substantially to building the church.*

for which he received a charter of confirmation, witnessed by Becket as Chancellor, in 1155. In the late summer of 1155 Bristol got its first Charter, confirming existing liberties. Another of Bristol's earliest Charters, of 1171, provided that the men of Bristol were 'given to inhabit' the city of Dublin, and made Dublin a form of trading colony. King John's Charter of 1188 reveals Bristol as a growing merchants' town which put business restraints on non-Bristolians. They might not buy leather, corn or wool from other 'foreigners' but only from Bristol merchants. They could only buy cloth at 'Fair times', and the stay of a stranger and his saleable goods was limited to 40 days.

Henry III built a new hall and gatehouse to the castle and it became one of the principal royal residences in England. From 1203 to 1241 Princess Eleanor of Brittany, remained a prisoner there. Richard I had wanted his nephew, Arthur of Brittany to succeed him as king, but John's henchmen murdered Arthur in 1203. To ensure that the young princess Eleanor, Arthur's sister, should not produce an Angevin heir to the throne to rival the Plantagenets embodied by King John and his son Henry III, Eleanor was imprisoned in the castle all her life.

Further Charters were granted to Bristol by Henry III, and it was during his reign that the growth of the port necessitated the creation of a new improved harbour by diverting the course of the river Frome. Such an undertaking was one of the most remarkable examples of civic engineering in England. The export of wool, cloth, ropes, lead, and sailcloths, and the import of wines, was clogging the port facilities. At low tide ships strained their timbers on the stony bottom of the Avon, and the quay was too small and inconvenient. The ambitious proposal was to change the course of the tributary Frome from just south of, and parallel to Baldwin Street, into a new and deeper channel across St Augustine's Marsh. This was accomplished between 1239-47 and

**10** *(above)*    **Bristol Bridge, built c.1239**
*The thirty houses and the Chapel of the Assumption on Bristol's medieval bridge survived from 1239 to 1764. The narrow arches restricted the flow of the river and created a weir effect. The shops established in the houses on both sides of the bridge were mainly jewellers and mercers by the 14th century.*

**12** *(below)*    **Dominican Friary, built c.1230**
*The Friary eventually came into the possession of Dennis Hollister, a Quaker grocer, Bristol MP in Barebones' Parliament 1653. It became Quakers Friars Meeting House. Extreme left is the Cutlers' Hall, originally the dormitory. In the right foreground is the Bakers' Hall.*

**11** *(above right)*
**Chapel of the Assumption of the Blessed Virgin Mary**
*The Chapel stretched across the width of Bristol Bridge. Over the gateway can be seen a portcullis which could seal off the town. The Chapel was largely paid for by the mayor in 1361, Elyas Spelley. The tower was 100 feet high and the structure included a Hall where the Corporation sometimes met.*

**13** *(opposite)*    **St John's Gate**
*St John's is the only surviving city gate. A gate and church terminated each of the four main streets of the early medieval city: St John's, St Leonard's, New Gate and St Nicholas. The old gates had grooves in the side in which a portcullis was let down. The other three seriously hampered traffic and were removed.*

involved spades and wheelbarrows. It cost £5,000 and provided a soft muddy bottom for ships to lie on when the tide was out. It was 2,400 feet long, 18 feet deep, and 120 feet wide.

On 27 April 1240 Henry III ordered the men of Redcliffe to assist in this project and to help build stone-faced quays on the town side. The city was hoping to win back some of the shipping then going to Redcliffe Back, and hence the reluctance of the men of Redcliffe to help. The new channel did much to establish the prosperity of the port in the following centuries as the new harbour was spacious. Redcliffe benefited at this time from a number of charitable

endowments from the Berkeleys on land owned by them. These included St John's Hospital, St Catherine's, Brightbow, and a hospital for women lepers at St Mary Magdelene, Brightbow (between Redcliffe and Bedminster). An older hospital for male lepers had been built outside Lawford's Gate and called St Lawrence's. Also the Hospital of St Mark's, known as 'Gaunts', was established across College Green by Maurice Berkeley de Gaunt, who was a grandson of Fitzharding, and by his nephew, Robert de Gournay.

The reign of Henry III also saw the coming of the Carmelites, the Franciscans and the Dominicans to Bristol. A hilly town like Bristol had plenty of sources of clean running water which served Lewin's Mead and the Franciscans to the west of St James' Priory, and also the Dominicans in Broadmead. There were a number of parish churches which existed within the town before Domesday Book but we do not know which ones. St Werburgh suggests a pre-Conquest origin, while St Peter's was the mother church of the royal manor of Barton Regis. Churches in the centre of the town, Holy Trinity (now Christ Church), St Ewen's, All Saints, and St Mary-le-Foro, would certainly have been early. The building of the new bridge and the walling in of the Redcliffe suburb on the Somerset side of the Avon were projects completed after the course of the Frome was diverted and the quay completed.

To sink the three new piers for the bridge the river had to be diverted, so a temporary channel was cut across from Tower Harritz, near Temple Meads, to Redcliffe Back. This ditch protected the new wall but left St Mary Redcliffe and Redcliffe Hill outside.

**14** *(above)*  **Plan of Bristol, 1479**
*This plan, measuring 4¾ by 6½ inches, was compiled by Robert Ricart, town clerk, 18th.Edw.IV (1479) in the Mayor's Calendar. The view has no value as a plan but is of earlier date than anything similar for any other city in England. It is of interest since William Wyrcester was measuring the city at this time.*

**15** *(centre)*  **St Werburgh's, 1860s**
*St Werburga had a Mercian name, and this was a pre-Conquest foundation in Corn Street. Edward Colston was particularly generous in his endowments to the later church. It was taken down and moved, stone by stone, in 1878 to a suburb.*

**16** *(top right)*  **St Peter's, 1960s**
*A Saxon church once stood here, close to the site of the first settlement. The walls of the Norman tower are six feet thick. The nave was mainly 15th century. It was the Guild church and there were many brasses, tombs and chantries in it. This church and Aldworth's house are Bristol's greatest losses from the Blitz.*

**17** *(below right)*  **St Mary-le-Port, 1860s**
*Sited in the heart of the town, St Mary-le-Port was of Saxon foundation. Bristol's main market was once held outside the church, hence St Mary at the Foro or Market Place. There was a tannery close by. The 15th-century tower survived the Blitz.*

**18   Church of All Saints, built c.1150 and
early 15th century**
William Wyrcester said the Guild of Calendars
kept the town archives in All Saints' church. Early
in the 14th century a disastrous fire in the library
destroyed many of the documents. Outside was
the Tolsey or covered colonnade, erected in 1583,
where merchants did business on the nails. Dated
from 1594, 1625 and 1631, the nails are now
outside the Corn Exchange.

**19** (above)   **St Stephen's Church**
St Stephen's parish was created as a result of the enlargement of the
town in 1239-40, when a new bed for the Frome was cut through
St Augustine's Marsh. The Shipward family rebuilt nearly all of St
Stephen's in the Perpendicular style, with a clerestory c.1470. There
are no transepts and no structurally separate chancel.

**20** (left)   **Edward Blanket**
Blanket was a wealthy clothier who lived in Tucker Street. M.P. for
Bristol in 1362, 36 Edw.III, he is shown here dressed in the civilian
attire of the time. He died in 1371 and his tomb is in St Stephen's
Church. It probably preserves the original level of the nave, and
interfered with the line of the new wall when the church was rebuilt
c.1470.

**21   Redcliffe Gate, c.1770**
*This gate had been an obstruction to traffic and was rebuilt in 1731 at a cost of £250. Eventually the inconvenience necessitated its removal altogether in June 1771. The porters at Redcliffe and Temple Gates received a salary of 37s. each per annum from the sheriffs, and lived in lodges by the gates.*

**22   Bristol's High Cross, 1373 and 1851-5**
*There had been a High Cross on the High Street/Corn Street site in 1247, but a new and splendid one was erected in 1373 to commemorate Bristol's county status. In 1633 another tier was added raising it to 39 ft. 6 in. Removed to College Green in 1733, it was sold to Henry Hoare of Stourhead in 1763. The photograph shows a replica.*

On the new bridge a double row of half-timbered houses grew up as on London Bridge. This bridge lasted until 1768 and its foundations are still there. The Redcliffe suburb was more extensive than the old town until Bristol began to expand north of the Frome. The suburb was required to pay 1,000 marks, the same as Bristol itself, towards King John's special subsidy in 1210. Bristol's pre-eminence meant that it had an important role to play in the conflicts between the barons and the Crown during Edward I's reign (1272-1307). Edward II was imprisoned by his Queen Isabella and her lover Mortimer in Bristol Castle in 1327, and was later moved to Berkeley where his dreadful murder took place.

Finally, in desperate need of money for the wars against France, Edward III in 1373 granted Bristol the status of an independent county and granted it a Charter, on payment of 600 marks. The period of

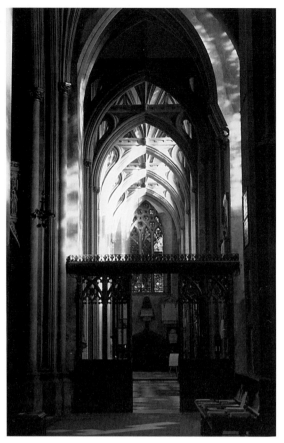

**23   South Choir Aisle, Bristol Cathedral, built c.1330**
*The choir limb of the cathedral is unique among England's greater churches. The designer managed to convey space because of the large windows in the aisles, which are the same height as the central vault. The outward thrust was transmitted to the buttresses outside by means of horizontal stone beams.*

the Charter, and of new county status, saw also a remarkable flowering of originality in architecture. The High Cross was erected in 1373 to commemorate the event at the intersection of High Street, Wynch Street, Broad Street and Corn Street. It can now be seen at Stourhead (on National Trust property). The choir of St Augustine's Abbey had been built in the 1330s as a 'hallchurch', with the three vaulted aisles of equal height, and with transverse beams withstanding the thrust of the main vault, thus creating a great sense of space. The almost complete replacement of the early St Mary Redcliffe commenced about 1340. In 1376 rebuilding was resumed from the transepts westwards and by 1400 the whole nave may have been completed. By European standards, Bristol was still a small town and could not compare with the great cloth centres of the Low Countries. It was no Antwerp or Bruges, but it was to have a great future.

## II

## *Wine, Woad, and Guilds*

In youre port the tydes of the see fallith bi course of kind every houre of the nighte as well as in the day at whiche seasouns the merchauntes secheth with all their crafte and witte to conveye their goods uncustumed …

*Great Red Book IV*, 90-91.

THE PORT'S PROSPERITY in the 11th and 12th centuries had been based on trade with Ireland, but in 1152 Henry II had married Eleanor of Aquitaine, opening up the whole of her duchy, including Gascony, to trade. In the 13th century wine dominated Bristol's commerce. Before 1200 the bulk of Bristol's wine probably came from Anjou and Poitou but, although Gascon wine is first mentioned in John's reign, and in 1250 Bristol Castle became a store for royal wine, it was probably being imported sometime before that. The Accounts of the Constables of Bristol Castle record the king's right to levy three pennies on every ton imported into Bristol by merchants who did not come from exempted towns. In years of peace imports of wine were more than 3,000 tons, and by the end of the 14th century Bristol was importing one-tenth of England's total. Only the ports of London, Southampton, and Sandwich imported more wine than Bristol.

The voyages took place after the vintage had been approved and therefore the mariners faced the usual storms and possible shipwreck. Piracy was also rife and merchants' agents could be captured and held to ransom, as was Thomas Canynges, nephew of William. Wine, as opposed to the common drink ale, was a luxury good and therefore the risks were

worth taking. After the loss of all French possessions apart from Calais and the Channel Islands in 1453, Bristol wine merchants imported more Spanish and Portuguese wine until, by 1500, Spain supplied one-third of Bristol's wine imports. Large-scale importation of sherry, however, was a feature of the city's trade in the later 16th century. Portugal and Spain also supplied sugar, cork, olive oil, almonds, honey, iron ore, soap and dye woods. From Bordeaux also came woad for the Redcliffe dyers and weavers.

After wine, woad, used for dyeing cloth, is the most frequently mentioned import in the 13th-century records. Wool exports were not of real significance at Bristol, although it was a Staple Town and although Bristol had easy access to supplies of best quality wool. The merchants of Brabant and Flanders preferred the shipping routes to our east coast ports. Hides, lead, ropes and sailcloth were exported in small quantities to Gascony and elsewhere, but cloth became the real basis of the town's maritime trade in the 14th century. Up to the outbreak of the Hundred Years War (1337-1453) no dominant export had emerged. A flourishing cloth industry had long existed in Bristol but producing mainly for the home market. It was the major harbour improvement in the 13th century that eventually led to Bristol and Redcliffe's rapid

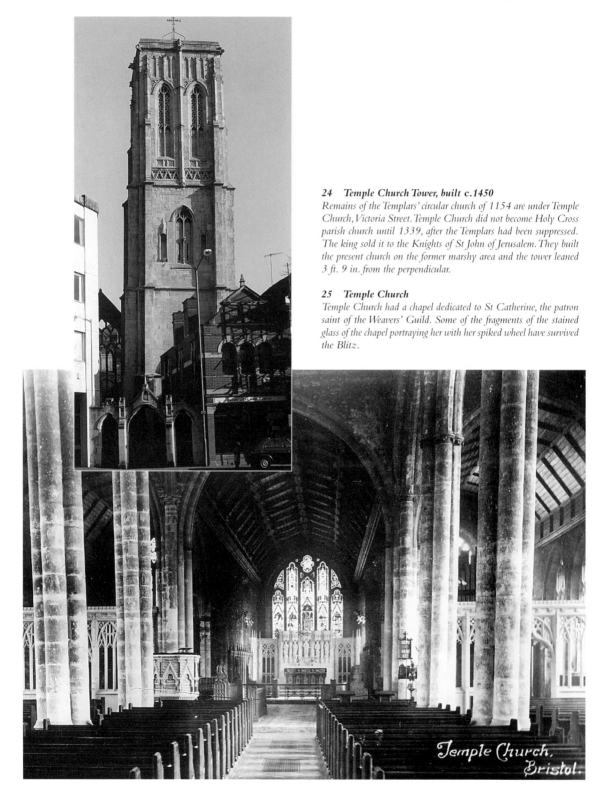

**24   Temple Church Tower, built c.1450**
Remains of the Templars' circular church of 1154 are under Temple
Church, Victoria Street. Temple Church did not become Holy Cross
parish church until 1339, after the Templars had been suppressed.
The king sold it to the Knights of St John of Jerusalem. They built
the present church on the former marshy area and the tower leaned
3 ft. 9 in. from the perpendicular.

**25   Temple Church**
Temple Church had a chapel dedicated to St Catherine, the patron
saint of the Weavers' Guild. Some of the fragments of the stained
glass of the chapel portraying her with her spiked wheel have survived
the Blitz.

expansion of that industry and the town became the cloth outlet for South Gloucestershire, the Cotswolds and Wiltshire.

By the close of the 14th century Bristol had grown far beyond the first city walls. Across the bridge over the Avon an industrial suburb had developed where many cloth workers lived. The cloth workers who had come to the 'Temple Fee' area, under the patronage of the Knights Templar, had left Abbeville in Normandy where they had lived by the river Toque. The area of Bristol where they settled was called Touker Street, later Tucker Street. A 'tucker' was one who processed (shrank or fulled) newly woven cloth and hung it on 'tenters' to dry. The Templars had arrived in Bristol in Earl Robert of Gloucester's time, and excavation has shown their early church, where the leaning tower of the late 14th-century Temple church now stands, was round when built. The Knights Templar were originally an order of warrior monks. Earl Robert had given them a grant of land known as Temple Fee. It was marsh land, and when the Templars were suppressed by the king in 1307, the site was taken over by the Knights of St John. The present structure was built in place of the original church and the tower was commenced in 1398. Built on soft alluvial soil, it tilted, but nevertheless in the mid-15th century the upper stage was added at a different angle. A weavers' chapel was built on to Temple church, and a Weavers' Hall was established in Temple Street. One of the wealthier weavers, Edward Blanket, who lived in Tucker Street, became one of Bristol's MPs in 1362. His tomb is in St Stephen's.

At this time nearly a quarter of Bristol's population was directly dependent on the cloth industry and until about 1400 Bristol was the greatest cloth exporting town in the country. It was to lose this eminence first to London and then, by the end of the 15th century, to Exeter. The reason for this change was the shift of the fulling operation to water-powered fulling mills in the countryside. Fullers, or

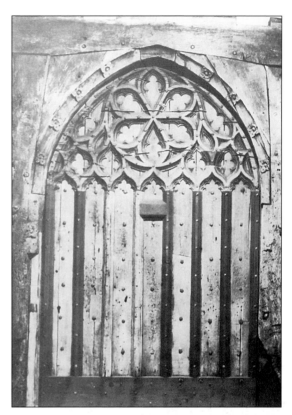

*26  Doorway of Spicer's House, Welsh Back, c.14th century*
*So little has survived of the wealth of domestic architecture in the late Middle Ages that it is fortunate that we have Spicer's splendid timber doorway. Spicer was MP for Bristol and three times mayor, and gave his house to the city in 1377. The doorway was removed in 1885 and is in the museum.*

Tuckers, in the Redcliffe Temple area lost their livelihood. Other occupations in the cloth making industry were affected by the new technology springing up near fast-flowing streams. Clothiers emerged who produced cloth, for export through London, in districts adjacent to the new fulling mills, and were able to circumvent the strict quality regulations of the Weavers' Guilds in the towns. In the mid-15th century Bristol Guilds attempted to halt this trend and to stop their members from dealing with cloth producers in the surrounding villages. They were unsuccessful and by 1461 the Weavers' Guild ordained that female weavers should be banned, except for Guildsmen's wives.

Divers persons of Weavers' Craft … occupy and hire their wives, daughters, and maidens, some to weave in their own looms and some to hire them to work with other persons of the same craft, by which many and divers of the King's liege people … goeth vagrant and unoccupied, and maynot have their labour to their living. (*Little Red Book*, Ordinances of the Weavers' Guild)

Tucker Street continued as a major cloth market each week, but the cloth now came from outside the town as well as being manufactured in Redcliffe, and was bought by the clothiers for export.

By 1450 there were more than 20 craft guilds in Bristol. These maintained quality standards, length of training in their craft, members' privileges, and

**27  Cloth Merchant's Brass, Temple Church, c.1390**
*This is Bristol's only brass from the time of the Charter of 1373. It was originally in Temple Church, in the main cloth-making district. It shows a man in civilian dress with close cropped hair. After the Blitz the brass was removed to St Mary Redcliffe.*

**28  The Horsefair, 1880**
*This open space was originally connected to St James' churchyard. In 1238 the Bishop of Worcester ordained that a feast of relics should be held yearly at the Priory of St James during the week of Pentecost. By Queen Elizabeth I's time these fairs were held on 25 July. The area is now the site of Bentall's, formerly John Lewis.*

represented their members' interests to outside bodies such as the town corporation or the Crown. They also had important religious functions. This was an age of faith when wealthy merchants showed a great desire to be benefactors. They believed they could reduce the time spent in Purgatory, after their death, by almsgiving to the poor, founding chantries where their souls could be prayed for, and endowing religious houses. John Barstable, for example, in 1395, founded the Trinity almshouses in Old Market. Many families contributed to the building of St Mary Redcliffe, including William Canynges the younger. By the 15th century, Bristol merchants had endowed and supported many chantries, religious houses, hospitals and churches. Eighteen parish churches were packed inside the city walls. The importance of the town as a religious centre is seen by the fact that the Dominicans, Franciscans, Carmelites and Augustinians all built religious houses around the town.

The town's burgesses benefited most from Edward III's grant of county status in 1373. They formed the elite who were able to buy and sell without toll or restriction. Forty of their number were chosen by the mayor and sheriff to become councillors 'with the consent of the community'. The mayor was chosen from among the councillors by annual election. The sheriff was chosen by the king

**29  View across St James' churchyard, 1826, by T.L.S. Rowbotham**
*The buildings beside St James' were part of the old Priory. In the distance is St Michael's, Kingsdown. For two or three days during the week of Pentecost a fair was held in this churchyard from 1238. The fair dealt mainly in horses, but also in cloth and leather. The stalls were roofed in wood and took about a month to prepare.*

*30 (top left)* **Candelabrum, Berkeley Chantry Chapel, Bristol Cathedral**
*Not many artefacts from pre-Reformation Bristol have survived. This is the only medieval candelabrum in England. It has the Virgin and Child above and St George and the Dragon below. It was given in 1450 to Temple Church and survived the Blitz.*

*31 (bottom left)* **North outer porch, St Mary Redcliffe, built c.1280**
*The doorway is cusped in a Moorish manner and the decoration has the appearance of silver-work which is quite unique. The outer porch is hexagonal, and is built as the crown to the shrine in the inside porch. Inside is the ancient relic house where the original iron grilles can still be seen.*

from a list of three candidates presented by the Common Council. By 1499 another Charter tightened the grip of this self-electing oligarchy, recognising an inner elite of five aldermen, one each for the five wards of All Saints', St Ewen's, St Mary-le-Port, Trinity and Redcliffe. These aldermen were Justices of the Peace, and one of them became the Recorder, or senior law officer. The number of sheriffs was increased to two. The effect of these changes improved the way law was enforced, but also tightened the grip of this small elite group on Bristol.

One became a burgess most easily by inheriting one's father's status on coming of age. It could be bought however by paying an entrance fee of £10, a very large sum equivalent to a year's income of a landed gentleman, and by being sponsored by two burgesses. Another avenue to becoming a burgess was apprenticeship to a master for seven years or more. Not more than a third of those apprenticed actually became burgesses. Not all apprentices had the necessary financial backing from parents or friends to set up on their own account and to take up their freedom. For example, John Whitson was apprenticed in 1570, but he was not in a position to become a burgess until 17 March 1585. Whitson

*32   William Canynge's House, 93 Redcliffe Street, built c.1300*
*Canynge's house, dating from the 14th century, was destroyed for road widening in 1937. It had a fine arch-braced hall roof, and the photograph shows the splendid woodwork. Edward IV dined in the banqueting hall of this great house in 1461.*

*33   William Canynge's House*
*This superb 14th-century fireplace depicts Canynge as a merchant on one side, and as Dean of Westbury College on the other. The fireplace has been preserved and cared for by the Bristol Savages, Park Row. In the alcove above the mantelpiece is represented the Judgement of Solomon.*

acquired the necessary business backing by marrying a rich widow.

The widow of Nicholas Cutt, alderman and merchant, was probably about thirty in 1585. Whitson had been apprenticed to Cutt and Bridget his wife, when he was 14 or 15 years old, on 29 September 1570. Aubrey's *Brief Lives* graphically describes what followed: 'He was a handsome young fellow, and his old master (the Alderman) being dead, his Mistress one day called him into the wine cellar, and bade him broach the best Butt in the cellar for her, and truly he broach't his Mistress, who after married him.' The parish register of St Nicholas shows that the marriage took place on 12 April 1585, and that the first child was christened on 2 November 1585, 204 days later. By this means Alderman Whitson got his chance to become a merchant on his own account.

The jurisdiction of the oligarchy that dominated the Common Council of the town was sometimes in conflict with the privileges and liberties of the Church. One dispute which lasted from 1491 to 1496 between the Abbot of St Augustine's, and the Mayor and Commonalty of Bristol was recorded in the *Great White Book*, and takes up the first 37 pages of that volume. The Abbot claimed to Henry VII that the Abbey precincts and its surroundings, which formed its area of administration, did not come within the jurisdiction of the town council. This area extended across St Augustine's Green to Gaunt's Hospital and St Mark's, and was part of the manor of Billeswick. In that area they could hold their own courts, keep all dues and fines, and offer sanctuary to criminals. The Mayor and Common Council on the other hand said the area had always been within the town, that the sheriff, coroner, and bailiffs had always exercised their authority there and assessed the inhabitants along with all other citizens. Townsfolk were incensed by the abuse of sanctuary by criminals who continued to indulge a life of crime outside. Underlying these issues it appeared the Abbot had

**34  Mayor Making Ceremony, Michaelmas Day, 29 September 1479**
*Robert Ricart, the Town Clerk, is the little man holding an open book below the mayor, Edmund Westcot, shown taking the oath. The retiring mayor, William Spencer, is administering the oath. Behind the new mayor and standing under the shield is John Shipward, who had twice been mayor in 1469-70 and 1477-8.*

increased the number of his mills from two to four and encouraged the townspeople to grind their corn in the Abbey mills rather than the town mills. He was also accused of taking wheat, barley and other grains, and exporting the greater part to Ireland, contrary to law.

The dispute culminated in a full-scale riot on College Green when the Mayor and his officers, at the king's command, sought out the vagabonds who had taken sanctuary in the Abbey, and were attacked by the Abbot's servants and monks. Accompanying the Mayor were the wardens of the Bakers' Guild and

others, numbering twenty-five or so, and the Mayor carried with him a set of scales to hold an assize of bread on the Green. This was normally held twice a year within the walls of the town. Any of the traders on the Green found selling short measure would have his bread confiscated and given to the poor.

According to witnesses produced by the Abbot's side, the Mayor's men ran amok, pulling down shopfronts, breaking into houses, and attacking innocent bystanders. Witnesses for the Mayor claimed the Abbot's workmen, employed on maintenance and rebuilding the church, and some of the monks, one armed with a pole axe, launched an unprovoked attack on them. The fracas temporarily ended with a public display of reconciliation by the Abbot and Mayor, the handing over of those who had claimed sanctuary, and the weighing of bread on the Green. It took the mediation of Cardinal Morton, Archbishop of Canterbury, and the Lord Chief Justice, to bring about a settlement.

Bristol was a town not only noted for occasional riots. It was significantly sceptical of priesthood, transubstantiation, and of the existence of Purgatory. At the furthest tip of the Worcester diocese along the north Avon, and administered in Temple and Redcliffe by Bath and Wells, Bristol was a particularly difficult place for either Bishop to control. As a trading and industrial centre it was open to novel ideas. Wycliffe, the 14th-century Oxford theologian, had a prebendal stall at Westbury College at Westbury-on-Trym. He taught that Purgatory did not exist, that souls were already predestined, that the mass did not change bread and wine into the body and blood of Christ, and that anyone, including women, could officiate at ceremonies and preach. Some of these ideas had motivated the Albigensian heretics in Langue d'Oc in the 13th century. Now similar views appeared in Bristol in 1384 when Wycliffe died. His disciple John Purvey settled in the Redcliffe and Temple area recruiting among the clothworkers. Like the Albigensians, the Lollards

**35 St Nicholas' Church, Bristol Bridge**
Robert, third son of Robert Fitzharding, gave the church to the
Abbey of St Augustine in 1172. The city gate was beneath the
chancel. The removal of the old gateway in 1762 entailed the
demolition of most of the church. James Bridges designed an ornate
assembly hall. The old crypt was preserved underneath the new
church of 1768.

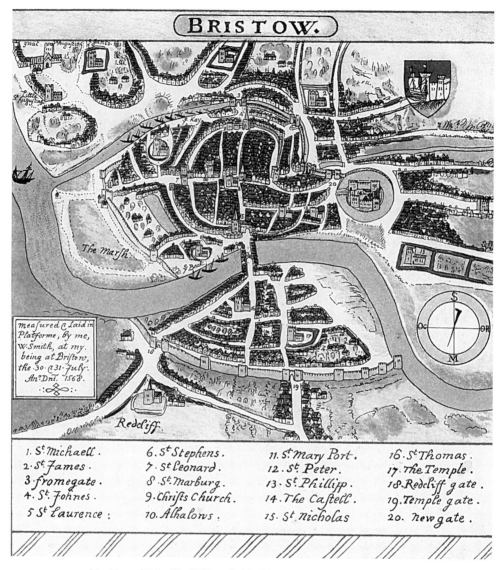

**36   View of Bristol by William Smith, 1568**
*(Sloane MSS. 2596, The Particular Description of England, 1588.)*

suffered persecution, and most preferred to renounce their beliefs, though some were martyred, such as William Smith. Such ideas continued to surface, and Bristol retained its reputation for radical thought until supplemented by 'Protestant' ideas from the continent in the 1530s.

The 14th century closed for Bristol with momentous political events. Richard II passed through Bristol in 1399 on his fateful journey to Ireland and on 4 July Henry Bolingbroke landed at Ravenspur. Richard's adherents took refuge in Bristol Castle where Bolingbroke, York, Northumberland, Ross, Percy and Willoughby sought them out and ordered the executions on 29 July of Bussy and Green. The event provided Bristol's one scene in Shakespeare's plays.

III

# *Voyages and Venturers*

BRISTOL IS BLESSED in many ways, and from the point of view of navigation the mouth of the Avon is naturally dredged. An eight knot current flowing diagonally across the Severn estuary scours it. North–north–east of Avonmouth the Severn flows through a channel called the Shoots, narrowed by a sheet of rocks known as the English Stones. This forces the river to act like a great natural dredger making a deep water channel with soundings of from six-and-a-half fathoms up to twelve. Nevertheless, in the 15th and 16th centuries, despite charts, the dangers of the Bristol Channel were considerable. The *Victoria County History of Somerset* (1911) describes it as 'a gulf with sands, islands and reefs, often swept by fierce and sudden north-westerly gales, chequered by furiously running tides and currents setting sometimes directly on to places a ship should avoid, and a seaway of which the navigation has never been well known to foreign seamen …' (*VCH Somerset*, ii, p.245).

Navigation, even today, is made more complicated by the range of tides on the North Somerset coast, reaching 41 feet at Avonmouth at spring tides. The effect on the river Avon is to reduce the river to a trickle at low tides, with a range of 37 feet under the present suspension bridge. The tidal range meant that Bristol had to be excepted from the Act of 1559 which had ordered that no vessel was to load or unload during the hours of darkness. After a petition, Letters Patent were secured from Queen Elizabeth in 1563 which stated:

the port of Bristowe is so dangerous and low of water, except it be at spring tides, that great ships laden cannot come nearer than four miles, because the water ebbs and flows suddenly for loading and unloading: whereby ships that before the statute might have been unloaded in four days cannot now be unloaded within 15 days.

Merchants trading abroad had many and great difficulties to overcome apart from the Severn and the Avon. Piracy was a profitable business, engaged in by Englishmen as well as foreigners. It was necessary for merchant ships to be armed, and they usually tried to sail together in convoy for their greater protection. The Merchant Venturers organised fleets to sail to the important continental fairs, and hired archers and gunners to fight off attackers. They also had to cope with the hostility on the part of foreign traders, especially those of the Hanseatic League. They sometimes had to face interference from the government at home, for then, as now, trade restrictions could be used as a weapon of policy.

In 1467 and again in 1500 Bristol's leading overseas merchants, trading in bulk, attempted to protect their interests by forming a trade guild of Merchant Venturers. They attempted to provide a supportive framework for members dealing particularly with Spain and Portugal, and to exclude those who were not specialist traders. What happened to these early attempts is uncertain. It was not until Edward VI, 1552, that they secured the first of the Charters preserved in their Hall today. Their 'Lamentable Representation' complained of interference in a trade monopoly by diverse artificers and handicraftsmen, destitute of mercantile experience, who had presumptuously undertaken to traffic in merchandise to and from foreign parts. Even with help from the young king all did not go well. In order to penalise small traders who were breaking their monopoly the Venturers obtained further confirmation from Queen Elizabeth in 1566, and from Charles I in 1639. It is the last Charter that the Merchants celebrate nowadays on 10 November, their Charter Day (unless the day falls on a Sunday).

The first building to be occupied by the Merchant Venturers was Spicer's Hall, fronting the Avon on Welsh Back. It was a 13th-century building and Richard le Spycer, three times mayor, and MP for the city in the parliament of 1355, bequeathed it to the Mayor and Corporation. The splendid doorway is preserved in the City Museum. The Merchants first met there in 1467, but they outgrew it and began building St Clement's, off the city centre, and met there from 1561 to regulate the sale of meat, oil, wool and wax.

By the mid-15th century some merchants were prepared to venture further than Spain and Portugal. From beyond the Straits of Gibraltar came exotic goods such as spices and silks, and as the Venetian hold on this trade weakened, some Bristol merchants like Robert Sturmy decided to take a risk and sail into the Mediterranean to trade. Sturmy, who had been mayor in 1453-4, left Bristol with three ships in 1458-9 and sailed past the Straits of Gibraltar to exchange wool, cloth, lead, tin and dyes for spices and peppers. These ships were attacked off Malta by several Genoese ships. The cargoes were stolen and Sturmy may not have survived the incident. Petitioned by the Mayor of Bristol, the king imprisoned all Genoese merchants in London until £6,000 was paid in compensation. This was a vast amount of money.

Bristol merchants certainly traded with Iceland, and we even hear, in 1479 for example, of voyages to Madeira for sugar. When Columbus went to

**37   A probable likeness of John Cabot's ship, the Matthew**
*This Caravel is 78 feet long, displaces 85 tons and needs a crew of 19 to sail her. It is now tied alongside Brunel's Great Britain. The ship was designed by Colin Mudie, cost £1 million, and was built by shipwrights on Redcliffe Wharf. It was launched in March 1996 and left for Newfoundland on 2 May 1997 to celebrate the 500th anniversary of John Cabot's voyage.*

Iceland in 1477, seeking information on what might lie beyond, he recorded that Bristolians were predominant among foreign traders. The Cabot voyages were thus not isolated episodes but part of a long process that, at the time, produced little commercial fruit. Following Columbus' success, Spain staked out her great claim in the New World and the Spanish Pope Alexander VI sealed it with a papal grant in 1493. However, John Day, who traded from Bristol to Spain, wrote to 'a Grand Admiral of Spain' (probably Columbus) about John Cabot's 1497 voyage, that the land John Cabot had seen 'was found and discovered in times past by the men of Bristol, as your lordship well knows'. This is a serious claim that Bristolians had discovered North America before Columbus, and the evidence of de la Cosa's map

(1500), showing all the English flags along the North American coast, seems to confirm it. It appears that from 1490 or 1491, annually for seven years, two or four ships sailed into the Atlantic on voyages of exploration, rather than commerce, though the amount of salt carried by some of them suggests it was new fisheries they were looking for. An alternative supply was needed after the Danish King monopolised the Iceland trade.

Atlantic voyaging had to be circumspect, however, and had to avoid areas of the New World which were claimed by Spain. Henry VII was intent on marrying his heir apparent, Prince Arthur, to Catherine of Aragon. Although the marriage treaty was signed in October 1496, there were five years of anxious waiting before the final ceremony. The Spanish ambassador, Ayala, was therefore consulted frequently by the king himself, before Cabot sailed on 2 May 1497 in the *Matthew*, with a crew of 18 men. On his return on 6 August, John Cabot was given a royal pension of £20 per annum from the local customs receipts, in recognition of his achievement. Other voyagers received similar payments in the same year. A small flow of Bristol traders then crossed to Newfoundland Banks fisheries. Despite Sebastian Cabot's great voyages into Hudson's Bay in search of a North West Passage to Cathay, little apart from the fisheries resulted from these first transatlantic efforts.

In the 16th century Bristolians built up their trade with Spain and Portugal, exporting tin, lead, metal goods, coal, hides and calf skins, corn, fish, butter and cheese. Cloth exports gradually declined from an average of 6,500 cloths in the last decade of the 15th century to 246 in 1600-3. (A 'cloth' was officially 24 yards long. On average, 84lbs of wool, or one quarter of a sack, was needed to make a broadcloth.) Much English cloth was unsuitable for southern Europe, and by the end of the century Bristol could no longer claim to be a major cloth exporting city. Imports of wine from France and Spain fluctuated with the wars throughout the century but remained an important part of Bristol's trade. By the end of the 16th century Bristol's trade showed a much wider spread than formerly. Voyages were made to Italy, the Near East, Madeira, the Canaries, and even to West Africa, and Bristol now received Dutch and Scandinavian exports.

For those mariners who ventured on the longer voyages the conditions at sea were atrocious. For centuries sailors followed a diet that was largely unfit for human consumption, consisting mainly of dried beans and peas, dried biscuit and salt pork. The ship commanders longed to make landfall for fresh water and fresh vegetables. Before a ship was more than a week out of port bacteria multiplied in the water casks. Even in Captain Woodes Rogers' newly built ships, towed out from Hung Road to King Road on 15 June 1708, and waiting for a convoy till 1 August before setting out for Cork, the water in the casks became putrid and undrinkable. Fresh water was obtained at Cork, but then the next stopping place was Tenerife in the Canary Islands. After that it was the Cape Verde Islands off the coast of Africa. Then came two months without stopping from 8 October to 30 November until the Falkland Islands were reached and fresh water could be obtained. The next regular stopping place for water was Juan Fernandez, off Chile and, depending on the time of year, the difficulty of rounding Cape Horn and sailing through the Magellan Straits might take three weeks to three and a half months. Lord Anson's fleet of six ships tried to round Cape Horn from 27 February 1741 through March and April and May, and *The Centurion* reached Juan Fernandez on 9 June. Over 200 men on board had died of scurvy. The *Tryal* arrived on the 12 June, having buried 34 men, and the *Gloucester* appeared on 26 June, and had to remain offshore for a fortnight for lack of crew, despite fresh water and vegetables rowed out to those surviving. Two-thirds of her crew had died of scurvy. Fresh men had to row out to bring the ship in. This illustrates the perils of those that set out on voyages.

Every nation tried to get hold of those few Atlantic or Pacific islands located along the main highroads of trade: St Helena was claimed by the Portuguese in 1502, seized by the Dutch East India Company, and then by the British; the Cape of Good Hope was occupied by the Dutch in 1652. Ascension Island in the south Atlantic and Mauritius in the Indian Ocean, half way between the Cape and Java were important fresh vegetable stations that regularly changed hands. The deficiency of vitamin 'C', scurvy, was the great curse. Scurvy affects the blood, causing haemorrhaging. It dries the gums and the teeth fall out, making it impossible to chew. One experiences fever, pains in the muscles, grippe and swelled legs. Old wounds, healed for years, break open again, and one has difficulty breathing. After a few weeks one dies of pneumonia or kidney disease. Given fresh vegetables, potatoes, apples, grapes, pears, onions or cabbages, the sufferer recovers within days.

On sailing ships there could be no regular hours. The wind waits on no man. Sailors were soaking wet most of the time, with no change of clothes, and could have gangrenous fingers from having their hands frozen. They lived in very cramped conditions. Sails shred, cordage freezes and snaps, men climb up rigging and get swept overboard. The ships are assailed by huge seas, violent squalls, and unfavourable currents in the Atlantic, or languish in unrelenting heat, without a favourable wind, off Africa. Bristol merchants in the 15th and 16th centuries were willing to risk their ships, and their men's lives, to open up new trading areas, new fishing grounds, or to find new routes to reach the spices and exotic goods that fetched such high prices in Bristol and the surrounding area.

There were other Bristolians, including Anthony Parkhurst and the younger Richard Hakluyt, who argued for more genuinely colonial settlements overseas, and from 1585, Hakluyt was a Prebendary of Bristol Cathedral. Parkhurst was one of Sir Humphrey Gilbert's backers on his voyage to Virginia in 1583. Secretary of State Thomas Walsingham suggested to Thomas Aldworth, Mayor of Bristol, that the city should back Gilbert's venture at a time when the Bristol merchants were more interested in the Newfoundland fisheries. However, in the year of Elizabeth's death, 1603, Martin Pring, backed by the Merchant Venturers such as John Whitson and Robert Aldworth, sailed across the Atlantic to New England and stayed there long enough to ensure English crops would grow in that part of America. His voyage followed that of Bartholomew Gosnold in 1602 to the Maine coast. Again in 1606, backed by John Popham, former Recorder of Bristol and then Lord Chief Justice, and also by Sir Ferdinando Gorges of Wraxall Court, Pring sailed to New England and explored the coastline. Nevertheless, as David Quinn rightly says, privateering provided more easily realised wealth, and 'the chances of a successful colony being established by the merchant-gentry group we must see as very small'. Anyway, the 'little ice-age' of the decade 1600-10 over much of the northern hemisphere, when the Thames froze over, helped to kill enthusiasm for settlement in New England for many years.

An interesting footnote to these early ventures was the return to Bristol of Martin Frobisher, from his second voyage to Baffin Island in 1577, with three Eskimos who astonished Bristolians by floating their kayak on the Backs on a duck-hunting expedition. Unfortunately they soon died from pneumonia. However Newfoundland still seemed attractive as a fishing base, and in 1610, John Guy, Sheriff in 1605, got permission from the Privy Council to establish a 'plantation'. He argued that it would supply this country with furs, timber, fish, whale oil from blubber, and ashes for Bristol's soap works. This early promise was not fulfilled, and although women went out among the early settlers, and the emphasis was all on a fixed settlement, the colony failed and Guy returned to England in 1613.

# IV

# Reformation, Civil War and Servants to Plantations

THE REFORMATION brought about momentous changes in Bristol. The skyline had hitherto been dominated by the Abbey of the Augustinian Canons, the buildings of the Carmelite Friars on the present site of Colston Hall, the Grey Friars or Franciscans in Lewin's Mead, the Dominican Friars in Broadmead, and the Austin Friars near Temple Gate. Also on St Michael's Hill was the small Augustinian nunnery dedicated to St Mary Magdalene. The oldest religious establishment was built near the Horsefair in the early 12th century. This was the Benedictine Priory of St James. Since the nave of the Priory had been used as a parish church since 1374, this saved it from later destruction. Although some of these religious houses, such as St Augustine's, were well endowed with lands bringing in a large income, others like St Mary Magdalene, were extremely poor and could only support two nuns. There was also a number of hospitals, such as St Mark's, known as the Gaunts, whose chaplains followed the Benedictine rule, and although they were charitable foundations caring for the poor and the sick, this did not save them from seizure.

When the Reformation Parliament was summoned by Henry VIII and began its meetings on 3 November 1529, few people could have imagined the vast changes that would sweep through religious institutions in the next few years. Within 10 years the religious houses had ceased to exist as such, releasing from Church control land for suburban development. Bristol became a cathedral city in 1542, thus continuing in use the Abbey of St Augustine of Hippo. These changes also incorporated the area south of the Avon into the city, thus ending the friction surrounding the Redcliffe and Temple areas where many of the cloth workers lived. The Reformation Parliament's legislation took place against a background of dramatic change which included the renunciation of the authority and power of the Pope in England, and the elevation of the king in 1534 to the Supreme Headship of the English Church. All monks and friars were ordered to declare their assent to this Act of Supremacy.

On 9 September 1534, the Abbot of St Augustine's and 18 canons, the Master of the Gaunt's Hospital and four brethren, and the Prior of St James and four monks, all acknowledged the Royal Supremacy. The friars took a little longer, or fled abroad, but eventually all submitted. Thomas Cromwell then sent commissioners out to assess the wealth of the religious houses and list this information in the Valor Ecclesiasticus which was completed by the autumn of 1535. Meanwhile another group of commissioners tried to discover evidence of scandal, laxity and failure of the ecclesiastics to live up to their ideals. Dr. Richard Leyton, who was the commissioner sent to Bristol in August 1535, had a hard job since there was no significant evidence of slackness. Nevertheless, reports from all over the country were enough to enable Thomas Cromwell in 1536 to persuade Parliament to dissolve those smaller monasteries whose income

*38 (above left)   **St Mary Redcliffe, built 1280–1380***
*St Mary Redcliffe lost its spire in a gale of 1445. This was not replaced until restoration began in 1858 when this photograph was taken. In 1872 the new spire was completed, and the mayor, alderman Proctor Baker, climbed to the top and laid the capstone.*

*39 (above right)   **St Mary Redcliffe***
*There was a church on this site in 1180 and parts of it are incorporated. It is the finest example of Gothic architecture in England. On 13 July 1588 Queen Elizabeth gave back lands confiscated by Edward VI to pay for its upkeep.*

*40 (far right)   **The Red Lodge, interior, built c.1590***
*The photograph is of the fireplace in the Great Oak Room. This is an exceptionally important representation of a late 16th-century house interior and has some of the most elaborate panelling in England. It was built by Sir John Young, owner of the Great House, and host to Queen Elizabeth in 1574. From 1854 until 1919 it housed Mary Carpenter's Reformatory School for boys and girls.*

*41 (below right)   **The Great House, St Augustine's Back, photographed c.1860***
*Sir John Young started building this house in 1568. Forty rooms were laid out round a rectangle. From 1654 till 1797 it was a sugar house. Edward Colston turned it into a school and Colston Boys' School occupied the site until 1861.*

was less than £200. That meant the end of the nunnery on St Michael's Hill, with two nuns and an income of £21 13s. 2d. per annum. The friars' buildings were closed in the autumn of 1538, freeing sites at Temple Gate, Lewin's Mead, the Red Lodge, Colston Hall area, and Broadmead. However, by 1538, St Augustine's, St James' and Gaunt's Hospital were still untouched. Two of these were seized the next year, in December 1539, by the new government department called the Court of Augmentations. Gaunt's Hospital and St Augustine's were surrendered on the same day. Finally, when the Abbot of

*42 (top)   **St Peter's Hospital, Aldworth's House, built 1612***
*Originally Norton's House in Wyrcester's day, this stood at the top of Castle Green behind St Peter's Church and is first mentioned in 1402. Aldworth rebuilt two-thirds of it and used the property next door, where the ladder is, as Bristol's first sugar refinery from 1612. It continued as a sugar house until 1695, then became Bristol Mint, then a hospital for the poor.*

*43 (above)   **Court Room, St Peter's Hospital***
*John Cary, merchant and churchwarden of St Philip and St Jacob, 1685, was of great importance in setting up England's first Board of Guardians under the new Poor Law in 1696. Their first meetings as a Court were held in the Guildhall but from 1698 to 1901 they met in this room in St Peter's. Here, for over 200 years, the Board of Guardians dealt with Bristol's destitute poor.*

Tewkesbury and 38 monks surrendered their Abbey on 9 January 1540, their daughter house, St James' Priory, also capitulated.

The Corporation of Bristol borrowed £1,790 and succeeded in obtaining from the king in 1540 the lands of the Gaunt's Hospital, those of the Greyfriars at Lewin's Mead, those of the Carmelites around the Colston Hall area, and a slice of land on St Michael's Hill, previously the property of the Magdalene nunnery. Royal servants, local gentry, and merchants who could find the necessary money to buy the former monastic lands, took the opportunity and acquired the rest. These included local gentry such as the Poyntz family, the Pophams, and merchants such as John Smythe, John Cutte, Thomas White and William Chester. The Corporation secured much of the purchase money by a deal with the parishes, whereby the chantries and parish churches surrendered much of their plate, processional crosses, and eucharist vessels in return for the Corporation abolishing tolls and dues on trade.

What happened to the monks, friars and nuns who were thereby dispossessed? Besides the two nuns at St Mary Magdalene, there was a manservant and a laundress. There is no evidence as to what happened to them. The Prior of the Austin Friars became the vicar of Bedminster. The Prior of St Augustine's,

**44    The Hatchet *inn, Frogmore Street***
*This building probably dates from the 15th century. It survived the demolition of Frogmore Street when the entertainment centre was built because it is on a traffic island. The inn has a small cobbled area at the rear and until the late 19th century it had a cockpit. The heavily studded framework of the entrance door is original.*

**45    *Bristol Grammar School Hall, c.1913***
*Robert (d.1532) and Nicholas (d.1546) Thorne, brothers who made their wealth largely in the Spanish Trade, believed Bristol needed a more literate class of merchants. They converted St Bartholomew's Hospital into a school and endowed it with lands in 1532. The school moved to Gaunt's Hospital in 1769. The Grammar School moved to Tyndall's Park in 1879.*

**46   Lewin's Mead, foot of Christmas Steps, c.1870**
Originally called Knifesmiths' Street, Christmas Street had been a precipitous footpath
until 1669. Alderman Jonathan Blackwell, a wealthy vintner, built proper steps called
Queen Street at his own expense. On the right is the entrance to St Bartholomew's
Hospital, founded by sailors c.1207.

Humphrey Hieman, became the vicar of All Saints', but the Abbot apparently went to the Isle of Wight with a sizeable pension. The monks found various parishes in the area, since they had local ties, and served as chantry priests at St Philip's, Temple Church, St Mary Redcliffe, St Thomas and St Nicholas, all with pensions. But the friars were not awarded pensions, and little is known about what happened to them. They received licences or 'capacities' to become secular priests, and mostly left Bristol. Three we know of obtained benefices in Somerset. These popular workers among the poor were allowed to disappear without any apparent opposition to their suppression, or voice raised in protest. Few in Bristol, of any persuasion, died for their religion. One of the chaplains of Gaunt's Hospital remained there as a parish priest. In the new cathedral, established in 1542, the top posts were given to displaced heads of religious houses. Bishop Paul Bush came from Wiltshire, where he had been Prior of the Bonshommes at Eddington. The Dean, William Snow, had been formerly Prior of the Austin canons at Bradenstoke, Wiltshire.

One priest, Edward Powell, backed Catherine of Aragon, denied the King's spiritual supremacy, and was executed in the Tower in July 1540. Five Protestant labourers were burnt on St Michael's Hill in Mary's reign, but Bishop Bush's successor, John Holyman, a former Benedictine monk from Reading, did not strenuously enforce Mary Tudor's drive against the Protestant changes. Under Elizabeth there were no executions of priests in Bristol. Hugh Latimer, who had preached Lenten sermons in Bristol in support of the new teaching in 1533, and stirred up opposition from the Prior of the Dominicans, John Hilsey, and from the Prior of St James, and the head of the Franciscans, later himself became Bishop of Worcester. Didn't Bristol care? Perhaps overseas trade with Spain and Gascony mattered more to Bristol merchants than a few doctrines here or there.

**47  Gaunt's Hospital, the Lord Mayor's Chapel, 1870**
*Surrendered to the king in 1539 at the Dissolution, the hospital was bought by Bristol Corporation. The buildings were used by QEH School, founded by John Carr, whitesoapmaker, from 1590. In 1769 QEH was removed by Alderman Dampier and the Corporation to St Bartholomew's. Bristol is the only city in England to have its own Corporation chapel.*

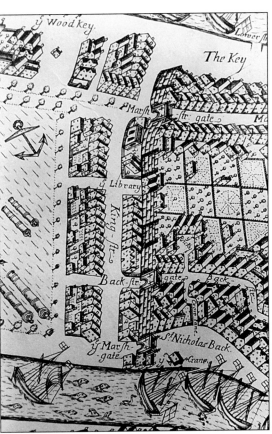

**48  Jacob Millerd's 1673 map, King Street**
*This shows the Merchants' Hall, the Old Library, high pitched gabled 17th-century houses and St Nicholas' Almshouses, leading down to Welsh Back. Much of this is recognisable today.*

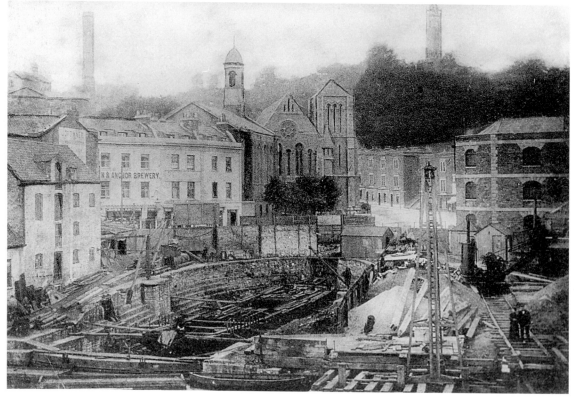

**49   Merchant Venturers' Almshouses, King Street, built 1696**
*The Guild of Mariners had existed in the 16th century and met in the Chapel of St Clement. With Edward VI's suppression of chantries in 1553, St Clement's was granted to the first Master of Merchant Venturers, Edward Prin. An almshouse and free school for mariners' children was built next to St Clement's and a new building was added in 1696.*

**50   Limekiln Dock**
*Built 1626 and demolished 1903, the dock was a natural pill below Brandon Hill, near the junction of Hotwell Road and Jacob's Well Road. By 1745 it had become a dry dock and was used by the Hillhouse Company and successors until the mid-19th century. Jefferies in 1882 fitted a new steel caisson and enlarged the dock.*

**51   St Nicholas' Almshouses, King Street, built 1656**
*The almshouse was built above a bastion which at one time was part of Marsh Wall defences. During excavations to build a new wing for flats in the late 1950s the old town wall was revealed. The building reopened in 1961 having been partially destroyed in the Blitz.*

A century later, during the Civil War, Bristol was besieged twice because it was considered by both sides to be of the utmost importance to their cause. On 9 December 1642 Parliamentary forces managed to occupy the city, although Bristol had tried to remain uncommitted on both political and religious matters as long as it could. In July 1643 Prince Rupert's forces recaptured the town at a cost of 500 Royalist lives. For the next two years Bristolians were subject to penal taxation and to forced labour in building three miles of fortified walls to the north of the city. The cost was enormous, but the value negligible, and Bristol surrendered to the Parliamentary forces of Fairfax after a siege of only two weeks, in August 1645. Through constant tax burdens, uncleared filth, the spread of plague, and the strain of billeting troops, the population of Bristol was reduced to desperate straits at the end of the year. The final fall of the city was the defining proof

**52   Tomb of Paul Bush, first Bishop of Bristol, died 1542**
*At the Dissolution Bush had been Prior of the Bonshommes at Edington, Wiltshire. The new See was wretchedly endowed and was regarded as the Cinderella among our cathedrals. Bush married in Edward VI's reign, was deposed by Mary for having done so, and retired to Winterbourne.*

**53 (below left)   Jacob Millerd's map, 1673**
*This part of the map shows the medieval city. Millerd was a mercer of Bristol and sold his map through Thomas Wall, bookseller. The castle site is covered with houses, and the ancient walls and gates, the High Cross, St Peter's Cross, and bridges across the Frome and Avon can be seen.*

**54 (below right)   Jacob Millerd's map, 1673**
*This part of Millerd's map shows the Back Lane and Jacob's Lane which were alternative routes when the market was impassable for traffic. It shows Lawford's Gate, New Gate and Castle Gate.*

of Royalist failure. It had become vital to the Royalists as an arsenal, a regional capital, and as a port of entry from Ireland and the West, when Plymouth, Lyme and Poole were securely in Parliamentary hands.

The siege of 1645 left Bristol under Parliamentary control, and there followed the 'purging' from the council of Royalists such as William Colston, Francis Creswick, Thomas Colston, Humphrey Hooke, Giles Elbridge, and many others. Royalist clergy such as Richard Standfast of Christ Church, and Richard Towgood of St Nicholas, lost their livings. Bishop Thomas Howell was thrown out of his palace. His wife, in childbed, watched the lead from the roof over her head being stripped off. It is thought that her death was the result of this. When John Evelyn visited the city on 30 June 1654 he

noted that the Castle, on the orders of Cromwell, had already been partly dismantled and Castle Street developed. Work was in progress on the parish almshouses for St Bartholomew's, in King Street. He was also taken to visit a sugar refinery, which represented an important element in the newly developing manufacturing industries of the city.

Immediately following the Civil War, Protestant nonconformists flourished. By 1652 a fully Baptist congregation broke away from Broadmead under Henry Hynam. Also in 1652, the earliest of Bristol's dissenting Congregations started in Castle Green. In 1654, following the visits of John Camm and John Audland, the Quakers moved into an upper room in Broadmead. In 1656 they were visited by George Fox, and also endured the antics of James Naylor who had parodied Palm Sunday and ridden into

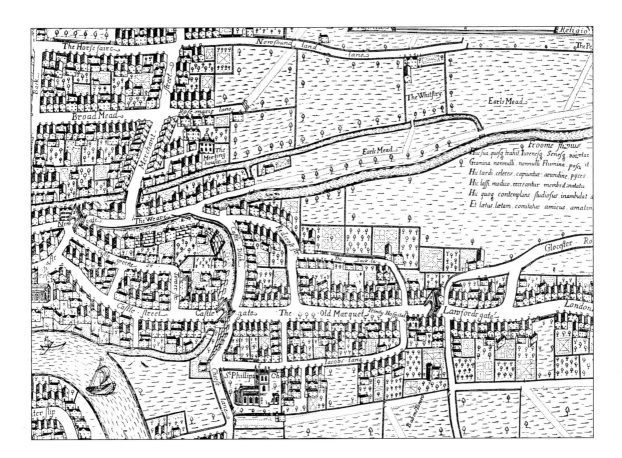

Bristol on a donkey on 24 October. Bristol saw an undoubted renewal of her trade and industry following the Civil War and slowly overtook Norwich as the second city of England. There were glassworks in Bristol in 1651, soap boiling flourished, tobacco had arrived from Montserrat in 1653, and there was a 'Delftware' pottery in St Anne's.

Bristol was a major embarkation port for the colonies in the early 17th century, particularly to Virginia, New England and the West Indies. The majority of Bristol's emigrants were poor and undistinguished, and probably most left as bonded servants. Others included political and religious offenders, kidnapped children, Civil War captives and, from 1718, common felons. After the Battle of Worcester in 1651, a large number of defeated Scots were brought to Bristol, merchants having negotiated with the government to transport them and others

**55 (below)   Jacob Millerd's map, 1673**
*Below Bristol Bridge is Tucker Street, the area occupied by the clothiers and weavers from the River Tocque in Normandy. It shows Rack Close where the cloths were hung out on 'tenter hooks', and at St Nicholas' Back the Great Crane.*

**56 (right)   Edward Colston's Almshouse, St Michael's Hill**
*This almshouse was built for 12 men and 12 women in 1691. The inmates were not to be 'drunkards' or of a 'vicious life', but those who lived in 'some sort of decency'. Each person in the house was to receive 24 sacks of coal and 10s. for soap and candles each year. The almshouse is now in the care of the Merchant Venturers.*

**57 (below right)   King Street, 17th-century houses**
*An 1890s photograph showing a smithy in the centre which survived until 1954. The first shop, no. 3, appears to offer palmistry for 1s. Next door, P. Nash has a clearance sale, but normally he soled and heeled ladies' boots for 1s. 6d., men's for 2s. 6d.*

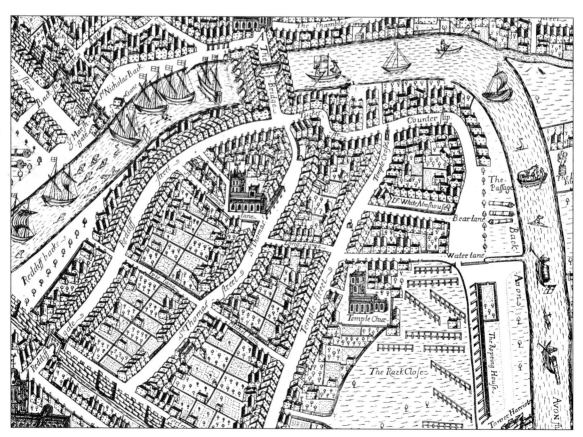

**58   Theatre Royal, King Street, 1766**
*This photograph shows the 1903 entrance designed by Pope and Skinner. The 17th-century houses to the left of the portico were demolished in 1904. The theatre was at the back and entered through a long tunnel. James Paty was architect of the Theatre Royal, which opened on 30 May 1766.*

from Chester, Ludlow, and Stafford to the West Indies and Virginia. There they were sold into slavery and died on the estates. Following the battle of Dunbar in 1650, of the 10,000 Scots taken prisoner, hundreds were shipped from Bristol to die as slaves. In July 1652 it was the turn of the Irish. The Council of State ordered the Governor of Waterford to deliver to three Bristol merchants, Robert Cann, Thomas Speed, and Robert Yate, as many rebel prisoners as they might choose to embark in their ships to the West Indies. Three months later Thomas Speed was given permission to ship 200 more to Barbados. Thus began Bristol's connection with West Indian slavery, and these slaves were all white.

Another source for labour in the colonies was by kidnapping, but on 29 September 1654 Bristol Corporation adopted a remarkable ordinance, similar to that already instituted in London's Parliamentary

**59   The Dutch House, 1676**
*Built as a residence for a wealthy merchant, this house stood on the corner of High Street and Wine Street from 1676 till 24 November 1940. In 1810 it became the Castle Bank, then in 1826 Stuckey's Bank. In 1855 T.W. Tilley, hatter, first called it Dutch House. In 1908 it was only saved from demolition by the Lord Mayor's casting vote.*

**60** *(opposite)*   **The Pithay, 1880s**
*William Smith's 1568 map shows the Pithay sloping from the upper gateway, fifty feet below Wine Street, to the Frome. In 1897 J.S. Fry acquired a great block of Elizabethan houses and demolished them to build new factories. Pithay comes from Puit-Hai, or well-close. The well was drawn by O'Neill for Braikenridge and was 50 ft. deep and 5 ft. across.*

**61   Llandoger Trow, *King Street, 1664***
*This inn is typical of 17th-century building in Bristol—gabled fronts, pantiled roofs, projecting bay windows originally filled with leaded lights, and display half-timbered work. Llandoger is a fishing village on the river Wye and a trow is a flat-bottomed barge. The inn was visited by Henry Irving, Kate Terry and Judge Jeffreys. Cellars beneath were used by press gangs as temporary prisons.*

Ordinance of May 1654, which was part of the general return to normality after the disruption of the Civil War. It attempted to prevent the 'Inveigling, purloining, carrying and Stealing away Boys, Maides and other persons and transporting them Beyond Seas'. For 30 years after 1654 every legally bound servant who left Bristol was entered in a book, *Servants to Foreign Plantations*. This records the place of origin, occupation, sex, age, name, master and the name of the colony for which the bonded servant was destined. This enrolment largely stopped when the black man began to replace the white man as the normal field worker on the tobacco and sugar plantations. However, indentured servants were still

**62  Memorial to Sir William Penn (1621-70), St Mary Redcliffe**
*Hanging on the wall are three streamers from his ships, his Admiral's crest, helmet, breast plate, gauntlets, dagger and spurs. The red flag of one of Cromwell's generals also hangs there. He captured Jamaica and was knighted by Charles II in 1660. He was father to William Penn of Pennsylvania.*

recorded as leaving through Bristol up to the American War of Independence, and during the years 1749-75, 3,279 servants went to Virginia and 707 to Maryland. It is not surprising therefore that Massachusetts and Rhode Island have counties named Bristol, and that there are nine or more Bristols in America.

Bristol had particularly close connections with Pennsylvania. Admiral William Penn had been sent out by Cromwell in 1654 to capture Hispaniola from Spain. He failed to do this, but seized Jamaica instead. This turned out to be of great importance to England's position in the Caribbean. It was not only a major sugar island but Kingston was the safest and

**63** *(above left)* **The 17th-century Seven Stars** *tavern*
*This inn is in Thomas Lane, alongside St Thomas' Church. Rev. Thomas Clarkson collected much of his evidence in 1787 on the slave trade here, enabling his friend William Wilberforce to persuade parliament to abolish the trade. Clarkson was much assisted by the landlord, Thompson.*

**64** *(above right)* **Fourteen Stars** *tavern, Counterslip, c.1856*
*The inn was pulled down in 1857 to make room for Conrad Finzel's sugar refinery. The inn was associated with sugar and rum, and was the resort of the masters of West Indiamen engaged in the slave trade. This is one of Hugh Owen's photographs. Owen was chief cashire for the GWR in Bristol, and an outstanding photographer.*

**65** *(left)* **A candlestick of 1712, Eastern Lady Chapel, Bristol Cathedral**
*This is one of two given by John Romsey, former Town Clerk to the Cathedral. They were given in gratitude for the successful privateering voyage round the world of the Duke and Duchess, 1708-11. Representations of the ships are shown on a medallion at the foot of each candlestick.*

most easily defended harbour in the West Indies. The Admiral is buried in St Mary Redcliffe. In 1681 Charles II settled debts he owed to Admiral Penn by granting 47,000 square miles of territory in America to William Penn junior and thus inaugurated the first Quaker colony in the world.

# V

# Slaves, Sugar and Tobacco

THE FATE OF PRISONERS taken at Dunbar, Worcester and Waterford is yet another instance of how greed drove Bristol merchants to ship white men to Jamaica, Virginia and Barbados. Bristol's involvement in black slavery from Africa to Brazil, to the West Indies and to the Carolinas and Virginia, is a horrific episode in the city's history. Some historians have tended to argue that these slave traders lived in an age with completely different perceptions, and that, by their lights, they were decent, honourable, God-fearing men doing a necessary job. Again, others argue, who are we to censure them from the perspective of the mass horrors perpetrated in the 20th century? It is undeniable that moral perceptions do change over time. Public opinion can be swung round quite quickly. The truth is probably that consciences had precious little to do with it. Bristolians made a great deal of money out of the slave trade and the sugar trade. While there was no incentive to change, other considerations could be argued to one side. It was said at the time, again and again:

> Different European nations have endeavoured to obtain a share in this valuable branch of commerce and particularly the French and the Spaniards give the greatest encouragement to it; and were this country to agree that it should be abolished, it would be eagerly seized on by other nations, deprive us of the benefit of fitting out annually a great number of ships, be a very great detriment to our manufactures, and terminate in the ruin of our British settlements

in the West Indies. (6 March 1788, Lords Commissioners of Trade and Plantations (M), African Trade, Report, pp.82-3. Printed in W.E. Minchinton, *Politics and the Port of Bristol in the 18th Century*, Bristol Record Society, Vol. XXIII, p.161.)

Between 1520 and 1570 the Ottoman Turks conquered Cyprus, Crete, the Aegean, Egypt, and much of North Africa. In so doing they extinguished most of the Mediterranean sugar industry since, unlike the Arabs, the Turks were not great traders. As a result sugar prices rose steeply after 1570, more than quadrupling, in real terms, in the last 30 years of the 16th century. Bristol imported sugar from Spain, which, in the Europe of 1600, was the only country producing in quantity, in the Azores. The Portuguese island of Madeira was a dependency of Spain from 1580 onward, and Bristol also imported from there. Though the Portuguese had since 1450 transported African slaves to Cadiz and Seville to work in the sugar fields and rice paddies of southern Spain, there was not a sufficient surplus to export them from Spain to the Caribbean. From about 1530 slaves were being sent direct from Africa to the Caribbean.

St Kitts, Barbados, Antigua and Montserrat were settled by gentleman-adventurers from England who took debtors, petty criminals and landless labourers with them as indentured servants, bound for seven years of bondage. After this, if they survived, they were free men, but debarred from returning to

who was Born a PAGAN and a SLAVE
Now Sweetly sleep a CHRISTIAN in my Grave
What tho my hue was dark my SAVIOR'S sight
Shall Change this darkness into radiant light
Such ... e to me my Lord on earth has given
... ommend me to my Lord in heaven
Whose glorious second coming here I ...
With saints and Angels Him to celebrate

**66   Scipio Africanus'
gravestone, Henbury
churchyard, 1720**

*Negro pages were fashionable in
the 18th century. Scipio was
servant to the Earl of Suffolk and
he died on 21 December 1720,
aged eighteen. His master, the
Earl, only survived him by two
months, and four months later his
widow Arabella, née Astry, also
died. There is no monument to
either Earl or Countess.*

Europe. There was no apparent reason in the 17th century for growing sugar 4,000 miles and three months away from the market in Europe except for the profits that could be obtained. Since the climate decimated the white servants in the Caribbean, an alternative labour supply was needed. Bristol's interest in Africa lay primarily in slaves, and not trade in goods. Occasional voyages to Africa from Bristol for slaves had been made illegally before 1698. These were in spite of the monopoly of the London-based Royal African Company. After the monopoly was ended in 1698 Bristol emerged as the major challenger, among the outports, to London for leadership in the British slave trade.

David Richardson has used the evidence of shipping records, customs accounts, and newspapers to show that 2,108 slave ventures were fitted out in Bristol between 1698 and 1807. He has found the mean loading of vessels was over 250 slaves during the 18th century, and that Bristol traders were responsible for carrying probably over half a million black slaves from the African coast. The total for all British ports was 2.8 million slaves, so that Bristol

carried about one fifth of them. By the 1720s up to 25 ships a year were setting out on slave voyages and between 1728 and 1732 the number rose to 48 each year. At this date Bristol had actually surpassed London as the premier British port concerned with the trade and accounted for almost half of the ships sailing to Africa. From this peak Bristol's involvement declined until her share of the British slave trade was 10 per cent on the eve of the War of American Independence. Although for most of the period 1728-32 slave voyages represented only 12 per cent of Bristol's shipping, the slave ships as David Richardson has shown, were generally larger and more expensively equipped than those employed in, say, the Irish trade, and the direct importance of slaving for the expansion of Bristol's overseas trade cannot be over-emphasised.

The death rates of the 'Middle Passage' to the West Indies were shocking. For 70 or 80 slaves to die on the voyage was quite normal. Two practices existed: the loose packers and the tight packers. Only the lure of big money kept it going because the risks from disease, storms, French or Spanish warships, mutiny, privateers, or shipwreck were considerable. When John Pinney sailed out to the family estates on Nevis, he wrote home to a Bristol friend in 1767, 'I can assure you I was shock'd at the first appearance of human flesh exposed for sale,' but he anaesthetised his conscience and pleaded, as did all the rest, 'But surely God ordained 'em for the use and benefit of us; otherwise his Divine Will would have been manifest by some particular sign or token.' (Richard Pares, *A West India Fortune*, Archon Books, 1968, p.121)

According to contemporaries, factors which assisted Liverpool's rise, and Bristol's relative decline in the trade, were Liverpool's lower shipping costs, and her willingness to supply illicitly to Spain's colonies. Historians have highlighted Liverpool's proximity to an industrial hinterland and relative remoteness from enemy privateers in wartime. Liverpool slavers were able to go round Ireland and to avoid trouble. Bristolians also, in time of war,

**67   *Lewin's Mead sugar refinery, built 1728***
*This is the only survivor of over twenty sugar houses in Bristol in the 18th century. The façade of what is now a restaurant is part of a complex of central courtyard, 100 ft. high chimney, boiler house and 'warehouse' next door. Although dating from 1728, this building underwent renovation in 1929. The 'warehouse' was where the boiling and cooling were done.*

preferred privateering, and by so doing lost markets. The failure to improve Bristol's port facilities, and the increasing times of turn-around, may have been equally significant factors. Also important was the growth of other outlets for capital and enterprise such as the sugar, tobacco, chocolate, glass, pottery, brass and copper industries. The return journeys in the Triangular Trade between West Africa, the West Indies and East Coast colonies, and England, brought in partially refined sugar, molasses, rum and tobacco. Bristol's first sugar refinery opened in 1612, and by the beginning of the 18th century there were twenty or more sugar houses in Bristol. Distilleries were attached to most of them.

Sugar became the most important ingredient of the city's prosperity in the 18th century. In the century or so down to 1820 cane sugar from the Caribbean was the most valuable British import. Intense competition with London and Liverpool in refining sugar resulted in some Bristol sugar firms going bankrupt in the period 1783-1812. Investment in steam processes and vacuum driers kept the industry alive, but from 1880 it declined and the last firm closed in 1908. Sugar refiners certainly made their mark on the life of the city. Between 1663 and 1832, 16 of them became mayors and 29 were sheriffs. Eight of them became partners in Bristol banks.

The decline in the industry was accelerated by the repeal of the protective Sugar Duties in 1846, and by the development of the continental sugar beet industry. Bristol dock facilities were far from ideal for enterprises needing to move large quantities of coal and partly refined sugar each week. It was not until 1881 that the Docks Committee tried to help the trade by reducing duties on imported raw sugar from 5s. to 2s. per ton. A further factor in the story of the decline of the industry was fire. Between 1670 and 1859 no fewer than 11 sugar houses were destroyed by fire, six of them in the 19th-century era of steam-driven processes. Ultimately, the Bristol

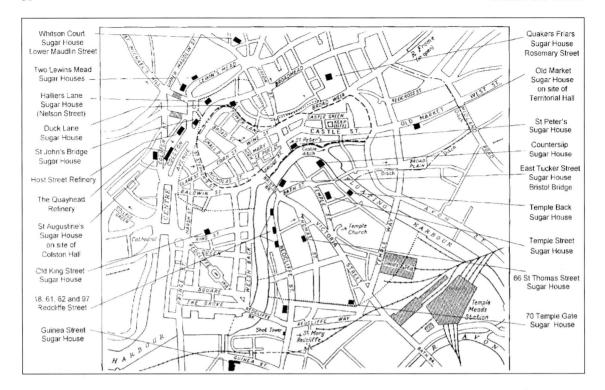

Whitson Court
Sugar House
Lower Maudlin Street

Two Lewins Mead
Sugar Houses

Halliers Lane
Sugar House
(Nelson Street)

Duck Lane
Sugar House

St John's Bridge
Sugar House

Host Street Refinery

The Quayhead
Refinery

St Augustine's
Sugar House
on site of
Colston Hall

Old King Street
Sugar House

18, 61, 62 and 97
Redcliffe Street

Guinea Street
Sugar House

Quakers Friars
Sugar House
Rosemary Street

Old Market
Sugar House
on site of
Territorial Hall

St Peter's
Sugar House

Countersiip
Sugar House

East Tucker Street
Sugar House
Bristol Bridge

Temple Back
Sugar House

Temple Street
Sugar House

66 St Thomas Street
Sugar House

70 Temple Gate
Sugar House

refineries were unable to survive, despite increasing the size of their operations and investing in new machinery. In Liverpool and Greenock the product had been transformed into handy cube shapes.

Just as, in 1698, Bristol merchants had to break the London monopoly of the Royal African Company before the city could become a major slaving port, so with tobacco London's Virginia Company had the monopoly from 1620 to import tobacco. Bristol merchants obtained occasional importing licences in the 1630s, but also grew tobacco illegally on a large scale in Gloucestershire. This enterprise was gradually eliminated by climate, poor quality of leaf, and by government action. In 1639 came official permission to import leaf through Bristol and several other ports. Samples of tobacco had crossed the Atlantic to Europe during the 1500s with Spanish and Portuguese sailors. Later in the century, English seafarers such as Sir Walter Raleigh, raiding Spanish territory in the New World, brought some back as part of the spoil.

**68   Map showing location of Bristol's sugar refineries**

**69   Fire at Old Sugar House, Tucker Street, 1827, by T.L.S. Rowbotham**
*The sugar refinery in Tucker Street, near Bristol Bridge, had ceased production in 1821, and was used as a warehouse. The toll houses on Bristol Bridge, the subject of the anti-toll riots of 1793, were used as shops in 1827. The view is from Dolphin Street. On the extreme left is St Mary Redcliffe, without its spire, and St Thomas'. George's Porter Brewery eventually became part of Courage.*

**70   Fuidge and Fripp, Quayhead refinery, 1859**
*On 30 April 1859, one of the most destructive fires recorded in Bristol's history destroyed the extensive sugar refinery of Fuidge and Fripp, near the Stone Bridge. £80,000 of damage was caused in money terms then. Two hundred and fifty workmen were put out of work and the refinery was never rebuilt.*

Cultivation of tobacco proved to be the salvation of the troubled colony of Virginia. At the Jamestown settlement which had nearly collapsed in 1610 from disease, famine, and hostile Indians, cultivation of tobacco was a money maker. Exports of timber, masts, dyes, furs, copper and iron ore had proved insufficient to sustain the settlement. The tobacco crop of 1618 was 20,000 pounds. Four years later, despite an Indian

attack that killed nearly one-third of Virginia's 1,200 colonists, the settlement exported 60,000 pounds. By 1627 the shipment totalled 500,000 pounds, and two years later that tripled.

For the English government tobacco became their richest source of revenue. Shiploads of colonists spread north to the Potomac valley and the Chesapeake's eastern shore. After the colony of Maryland was founded in 1634, tobacco quickly became its chief money earner, and leaf became legal currency in both Maryland and Virginia. By the end of the 17th century tobacco culture dominated an area from the southern boundary of Pennsylvania to the northern tidewater area of North Carolina. However, because tobacco sapped the soil's fertility, the quest for new lands exerted one of the early pressures for America's westward expansion.

Through most of the 17th century white English servants were the primary source of labour in the tobacco colonies. The price these emigrants paid for passage to Virginia and Maryland, as to the West Indies, was from seven to 15 years of labour for the planters who bought their contracts. The earliest mention of Africans purchased at Jamestown came in 1619 when John Rolfe wrote, 'About the last of August came in a Dutch man-of-warre that sold us 20 Negars.' Subsequently planters imported increasing numbers of black men from the West Indies, until by 1708 Virginia had 12,000 and by 1730, 30,000. In Maryland, the number of black men rose from about 8,000 in 1710 to 25,000 in 1720. By the end of the 18th century Virginia and Maryland had more than 395,000 black men and women. British tobacco imports increased as a result from 38 million pounds in 1700 to 100 million pounds in 1771-5. Bristol merchants by the 1690s were accounting for about 10 to 15 per cent of the trade. But, as with sugar, tobacco imports by the middle of the 18th century moved gradually to Glasgow, Liverpool and Whitehaven, which increasingly re-exported to northern Europe. After

the War of American Independence the number of Bristol firms involved in importing tobacco declined into single figures.

Tobacco, sugar and slave merchants were largely discrete groups in Bristol, and whereas sugar importers belonged to a fairly close-knit group of families, most tobacco merchants remained in the trade for relatively few years, and there was little family continuity between one generation of tobacco importers and the next. Substantial working capital was required to participate in the tobacco trade. Bristol merchants extended credit first to establish and then to maintain relations with clients on the Chesapeake. Poor prices for tobacco and a restricted supply of money meant that many planters were heavily indebted to Bristol merchants. By 1776 around £2 million was owed by Virginia, North Carolina and Maryland to British merchants. The outbreak of hostilities resulted in substantial losses, and a number of bankruptcies occurred among Bristolians engaged in this trade.

Snuff was the most significant of the products made from tobacco in the Bristol area in the 18th century, and many corn mills were converted into snuff mills. It is alleged that in an average gentleman's family, one pound of snuff was consumed each week in the mid-18th century. To set up a snuff business did not require much capital. The Clifton Observatory was originally a windmill for snuff, which was gutted by fire during a gale on 30 October 1777. Even during the War of American Independence there were 19 snuff makers and tobacconists in Bristol. Other tobacco products were cut tobacco and roll tobacco. Snuff mills existed at St James' Back, Territt's mill, Lock's mill, Coombe Dingle, Barrow, Frenchay, and there were two on the Frome.

Henry Overton Wills, the founder of W.D. and H.O. Wills, began business in Bristol not earlier than 1786, nor later than 1788. In the local papers of 1789 the firm of Wills, Watkins and Co. is mentioned. There were seven other tobacco manufacturers in Bristol

**71   H. and T. Proctor's glass cone, c.1925**
*Glass houses were very conspicuous, their cones being about 90 feet high and diameter inside 50 feet. The Prewitt Street glass cone was taken over in 1812 by H. and T. Proctor for the manufacture of chemicals and artificial fertilisers.*

at that time. These small Georgian concerns employed only a few workers each. Among the many other employers of labour at that time were over 40 brewers and maltsters, 35 vintners and importers of wine, and seven firms still making soap. Window glass and bottle glass making created work in 1793 in at least a dozen glassworks, and glass cone furnaces were a feature of the skyline. Copper and brass manufacture and zinc smelting were concentrated near the coal pits and by

the river where barges could reach them. In St Philip's were iron foundries making anchors, chains and cannons. To supply these industries the coal mines of Kingswood and Bedminster employed well over 1,000 men. In addition to these industries was one, drawing its raw material from the West Indies, and with small beginnings, which, like tobacco, eventually gave employment to thousands. This was the chocolate and cocoa industry.

During the early 17th century, chocolate found its way to Italy and England from Spain, where it had been introduced when Columbus returned in 1502 from his fourth voyage. Spaniards had learnt how to use the bean from the Aztecs, but the formula of how to convert the bitter bean into a sweetened drink was kept a secret for the benefit of the Spanish nobility for 100 years. In England it was manufactured by apothecaries. Joseph Fry, a Quaker apothecary, bought the patent, in 1761, of 'an engine' to manufacture chocolate, from the son of Walter Churchman. Joseph Fry had come to Bristol from Sutton Benger in Wiltshire and became a freeman of the city in 1753. His son, Joseph Storrs Fry, is believed to have been among the first to use steam in the process. In 1793 the business moved to Union Street but only employed 11 people at that time.

Increasing mechanisation permitted greater variation in chocolate devised as sweets. Conrad Van Houten, a Dutch chemist, invented a cocoa press in 1825 that enabled confectioners to mix cocoa butter with finely ground sugar to produce chocolate bars. A Swiss candymaker, Daniel Peter, added condensed milk to chocolate liquor to develop milk chocolate. As the market for sweets grew so did Fry's business. He employed 350 people in 1866, 1,000 in the 1880s, and by 1908 reached 4,600.

The cultivation of sugar cane and tobacco in the West Indies and the Chesapeake provided the engine of growth which had enabled Bristol to become England's second city by the end of the 18th century. Famous local families such as the Eltons, the Farrs, the Hobhouses, the Fishers and the Pinneys, that had grown wealthy through the slave trade and plantation servitude, gradually withdrew from the business. When an Anglican deacon, Thomas Clarkson, came to Bristol in 1787 to make enquiries for the Abolition Committee he found strong support from the Quaker banker Harford, and Dr. Fox among others. By 1787 Bristol's involvement in the slave trade was much diminished, and although the West India Committee, the Merchant Venturers, and the City Council continued to oppose abolition, the position was greatly changed. By 1807, the year the trade in slaves was abolished in the British Empire, Bristol ships carried perhaps ten per cent of the slaves. Bristol was no longer as convinced as thirty years previously of the necessity of slavery to local prosperity. At this stage they were not in favour of the abolition of slavery itself, without which, it was believed the sugar trade with the West Indies would be decimated. However, the painstaking detail of Clarkson's enquiry had revealed the sufferings of Bristol seamen, as well as slaves, and this had changed the climate of opinion. By the turn of the century, perhaps, the Abolitionists were pushing at an unlocked door.

VI

# Georgian Bristol: Merchants and Methodists

BY THE END of the 17th century Bristol had developed as a maritime trading city and, except for London, was fast becoming England's leading port. The Merchant Venturers' Wharfage Accounts, beginning on 4 May 1654, demonstrate the gradual growth in the number of hogsheads of muscovado

sugar and leaf tobacco imported into Bristol, and reveal the increase in shipping that resulted. Each voyage involved many people, not just the merchants who speculated in the venture. Investors were not all rich merchants, and many people invested a small amount in a container of trade goods. Shipbuilding, fitting out and repairing involved many joiners, carpenters and shipwrights. Traders supplied the ammunition, food and stores. Manufacturers supplied the Guinea pots, Guinea kettles, Manillas, iron bars, beads, mirrors, sail cloth and rum. There were those who fetched and carried about the port, worked on iron anchors and slave chains, made copper sheathing, brass fittings, or produced rope. Industries that processed goods for re-export to Europe also provided work for many people. There was an increasing demand for domestic servants and the need for apprentices, and as a result of all these factors Bristol's population trebled in the 18th century.

A key figure in the transition from the 17th century to the Georgian Age was Edward Colston (1636-1721). His father, William Colston, had been one of Robert Aldworth's apprentices, in the most exclusive set of Bristol's merchant community. Edward Colston made his fortune as a merchant in

**72   Edward Colston's statue, erected 1895**
*Edward Colston was one of Bristol's most famous benefactors. He gave the city the equivalent of £13.5 million in present-day money. He was born in Temple Street in 1636 but spent most of his life in London. He made his money as a merchant, and became Deputy Governor of the Royal African Company. He had a large interest in the slave trade.*

**73   Abraham Isaac Elton's house, built c.1753**
*Abraham Isaac was a lawyer and town clerk. His heirs sold his house in 1877. In 1950 two unmarried daughters of P.J. Worsley sold it to the University. Abraham Isaac was grandson to the first baronet, who died in 1728 leaving a vast fortune of £100,000.*

**74   Paul Fisher's House, Clifton Hill House, built 1747**
*The architect of Clifton's most distinguished house was Isaac Ware; the mason and carver was Thomas Paty. Fisher (senior, d.1735) had been involved in trade, privateering and slaves, selling to the American Colonies and to Europe. Fisher (junior) was also a merchant.*

London before returning in middle age to his native city to concern himself with social and moral reform. He had been born in Temple Street, the eldest of 11 children. He trained as a mercer in London, and traded with Spain and Portugal in wines, oil, Mediterranean fruits, and in sugar from the West Indies. From 1680 he was a member of the Royal African Company and heavily involved in the Company's administration, eventually becoming Deputy Governor, 1689-90.

**75 Aerial view of Clifton Terraces, built c.1787–93**
*None of these terraces that step down from the Observatory Tower are among Clifton's finest. The crescents that seized the steep slopes and scenic views were built by small building firms.*

Colston is commemorated now in the names of various streets, the main concert hall and two almshouses, as the founder of three schools, and by a statue in the middle of Colston Avenue. Sadly, his involvement in the slave trade, together with the prominence of his name around the city, have made him a controversial figure today. His statue was defaced in January 1998. Leaders of the black community have focussed some of their condemnation on him because he gave immensely generous benefactions to many institutions in Bristol but did nothing for black slaves. He died at 84, a difficult and cantankerous bachelor whose ideas mirrored those of the ruling elite at that time. He was a High Anglican Tory, a governor and benefactor of Christ's Hospital School, whose most costly gift to Bristol was the founding of Colston School on similar lines in 1706. Sixteen years earlier he had conceived and endowed the Colston Almshouse on St Michael's Hill, and in 1695 had rebuilt the Merchant Venturers' Almshouse.

Colston's school opened in 1710 with 100 boys whose dress was closely modelled on the costume of Christ's Hospital. In the same year he founded a charity school (Temple Colston) in the parish of his birth. He spent money embellishing All Saints' Church, Temple Church, St Mary Redcliffe, St Werburgh's and the cathedral. Yet, throughout, his charities exhibited an intolerant insistence on Anglicanism. Boys at his schools had to be Anglicans and boys apprenticed from Temple Colston could not be apprenticed to Dissenters. He was one of Bristol's two Tory MPs in the notorious Parliament of 1710-13 which passed the Schism Act forbidding any nonconformist schools, and giving the Anglican church an education monopoly. Fortunately it only remained on the statute book for five years and was largely ignored.

Other merchant families that played a leadership role during the critical century in Bristol's history included the Eltons, the Fishers, the Ames, the Brickdales, the Millers, the Hobhouses, the Farrs, the Carys, the Miles, the Champions and the Goldneys. Through privateering, shipping, slaving, trade and subsequently banking interests, they achieved considerable wealth over two generations. They formed a close-knit community and sometimes forged ties through marriage. Some of them, through the Society of Merchant Venturers, played an active part in formulating Bristol's trade policies as well as overseeing the port. Most of these families were involved in the slave trade in some way, and in privateering. Windfall profits for the few attracted much speculative investment into such ventures, and it was the successful families in this lottery who were able to build the splendid mansions which made Clifton such an attractive place.

This desire to move out of the stench, smoke and sewage of the old city to the fresh air of Clifton is one aspect of the fact that the century of Bristol's great economic growth saw significant physical expansion on the ground. The first extension was the reclamation in 1699 of the Marsh and the building of Queen Square, named after Queen Anne's visit in 1702. Then came a sequence extending eastwards from St James' Square, Portland Square and King Square. Above the city stench, Kingsdown and the crest of St Michael's Hill were developed. For a time the 76°F Hotwells were exploited along the Avon, but, at the end of the century, Thomas Morgan drilled a shaft 250 feet through the limestone to tap another spring. This yielded 34,000 gallons of hot water daily and permitted the building of a new Pump Room and hot baths in Upper Clifton where the *Clifton Rocks Hotel* now is. To the south there were also extensions to Redcliffe and to Bedminster.

The previous chapter has stressed the importance of the West India connection to Bristol. It was the factor that made the difference between Bristol being the chief provincial market centre for the south-west, and being England's second city. Bristol's merchants now ventured to Venice and Genoa, to

**76   The river Frome from Stone Bridge, 1826, by T.L.S. Rowbotham**
*Stone Bridge, where Colston's statue and the old Central Electricity House stood, was the highest navigable point of the Frome. Here trows containing coal from Staffordshire or the Forest of Dean were unloaded. Cider was sold here as well as at Welsh Back. The covering over of this area to the junction of Clare Street and Baldwin Street began on 11 May 1892 and was finished on 6 May 1893.*

the Baltic, to Riga and Petersburg, to Norway and to Newfoundland. Over 1,000 coastal vessels used the port, and perhaps 100 Severn trows. Probably no more than 30 of these coasters were Bristol-owned, but the expansion of trade meant the port became congested. Some of the trows were 60 feet long and weighed 100 tons, tapping a hinterland as far as the Potteries. The trows were able to navigate the Severn past Worcester, Stourport for the Black Country, and to reach Shrewsbury. They also sailed down the Avon to Bath.

Throughout the century port problems were in the forefront of merchants' minds and various improvements were suggested. Four to five hundred ton ships usually lay off King Road or Hung Road, where cargoes were unloaded into lighters and taken up the Avon. Ships that did come up to the city had to be towed by fleets of rowboats. Twice daily ebbing

of the water in the Avon and Frome was inconvenient for the loading and unloading of ships. Although quays were improved and extended, these were the days when the rivers were used as sewers, and the port was not a pleasant place in which to work.

By 1712 tide-free berthing was achieved at Sea Mills, as in Roman times. Also, and only a mile from the city, in 1767 William Champion constructed a dock, later called the Merchants' Dock, which took 16 ships. It was subsequently purchased by the Merchant Venturers who ensured it would be fully

**77   Old Floating Dock, Hotwell Road, 1827, by T.L.S. Rowbotham**
*This dock, now called Merchant's Dock, together with two graving docks (dry docks for cleaning and tarring), were built in 1765 by William Champion, near his house shown in the left foreground. He sold this dock to the Merchant Venturers and they enlarged it to take 16 ships. To ensure that it would be fully used they obtained an Act of Parliament compelling all vessels with a cargo of timber, tar or pitch, to offload on their wharf, away from the city.*

**78   A dry point etching of the Merchants' Hall by G.Willis Paige, 1933**
*Twice hit by bombs during the Second World War, on 6 December 1940 and 8 May 1941, this building stood on the corner of King Street near Broad Quay.*

used by obtaining an Act of Parliament compelling all vessels with tar, pitch, deals and combustibles, to offload on a wharf on the west side of this dock and away from the heart of the city. There were several dry docks for repair work, Tombs' in Canons' Marsh, two near Merchants' Dock, and one at Limekiln Lane, but these did not solve the major problems of the effect of the tides within the city itself. The solution was to come at the beginning of the next century with a major engineering work of 1804-9 through Rownham Meads.

Underlying most of Bristol's industries during the 18th century, whether glass, pottery, brass, sugar refining, lead smelting or iron work, was the use of coal. The nearness of the coalfield meant comparatively cheap fuel, and gave Bristol the edge over some northern industrial towns at first. J.U. Nef has suggested that by 1800 the Somerset and Kingswood coalfields between them produced 300,000 tons a year. The Duke of Beaufort's mines were as deep as 600 feet, and were the key to Bristol's glass, china, sugar and metal industries. In Soundwell there were three mines about 1,250 feet deep. In addition there were many 'works' or small mines, and 'pits'. Miners lived remote, semi-civilised lives, and their economic problems sometimes led to riots.

Coal was needed, for example, at Acraman's Anchor and Chain works, at Watt's Patent Shot works at Redcliffe, at the Bristol Brass Wire company, started in 1702 at Baptist Mills, and at William Champion's Warmley Brass Company, started in 1746. The Temple Back Pottery in Water Lane needed coal from 1683, and several other potteries existed in Bristol at this time. Glasshouses were conspicuous landmarks because of their tall cones sometimes 90 feet high, with diameters of 50 feet, and Millerd's map of 1710 shows their sites. In 1698 there were six making bottles and four more making flint glass. By 1722, according to Defoe, there were 15 glasshouses and, by 1794, according to *Matthews' Directory* 'about

twelve', each with several furnaces. So much glass was exported to the West Indies and to the American colonies, to the Netherlands and to the Mediterranean, that the industry provided work for several hundred workers.

Bristol had been a pioneering soapmaking centre from early medieval times. By 1722 there were 62 freemen listed as soapmakers or soap boilers. Among the famous ones in the 18th century were John Vaughan, the banker, Samuel Fripp, John Farrell, William Jones (Master of the Merchant Venturers in 1770), and Joseph Fry ( who had his own chocolate business.) By the end of the century Bristol was the third largest soap-producing centre in the United Kingdom. Of the total of 45,000 tons in the 1820s, London accounted for 15,000 tons, Liverpool for 8,500 tons and Bristol for about 3,600. The factories needed to be close to the river because of the transportation of coal, wood ash, tallow, alkali for the burning of kelp, and quicklime, all needed in soapmaking.

Metal industries such as pin-making, iron founders making anchors, ships' cannon and chains, lead shot making, and the forging and manufacture of brass also needed to be close to the river where barges could reach them. These industries tended to be sited in St Philip's, Redcliffe and Crew's Hole, and there were 81 furnaces at Warmley and Crew's Hole in 1754, for example. The Mendips provided the calamine from areas such as Shipham and Rowberrow, yielding the zinc mixed with copper in brass making. Copper ore came by sea from Cornwall. Breweries also needed to be close to the river, because they also required large quantities of coal. In 1793 there were over 40 brewers and maltsters in Georgian Bristol, perhaps the best-known brewery being built near Bristol Bridge by a group of merchants that included Isaac Hobhouse. It came in 1787 into the hands of a partnership managed by Philip George and eventually became the largest brewery in the West Country.

**79   Clifton from Rownham Meads, c.1800**
*These fields are now the Cumberland Basin. On the hill can be
seen Goldney's tower, the line of mature yews in the garden, Prospect
House, and the Chesterfield. In the foreground to the left stands the
Assembly Room which was demolished in 1963 for the Cumberland
Basin flyover.*

The miners who provided the coal for all these
industries lived in remote communities where,
according to Eden's *State of the Poor*, they 'speak a
jargon that is peculiar to them, and perfectly
unintelligible to a stranger'. George Whitefield's
mother was a Bristolian, and, after a period of
missionary work in Georgia, where he was
accustomed to open-air preaching, he returned to
Bristol and, from February 1739, preached to large
crowds of miners' families. Since Whitefield was
debarred from Anglican pulpits, he asked John Wesley
to join him, and from 31 March 1739 until
December, Wesley stayed in Bristol. On 2 April he

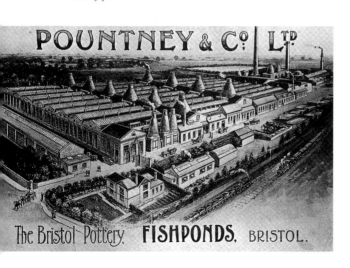

**80   Pountney's Bristol Pottery, 1905**
*Pountney's works began in 1750 near Temple Church. The firm
moved to St Philip's Marsh in 1884 and then to Fishponds in
1905. The works extended over eight acres and closed in 1969.*

preached his first open air sermon in a brickfield in St Philip's Marsh. Over the next few weeks he laid many of the foundations for organised Methodism. Between 1739 and 1742 he preached in several Bristol parish churches, at Lawford's Gate Poor House, and at the city gaol at Newgate.

Perhaps one-fifth of the 20,000 inhabitants of Bristol at that time were Dissenters, including Quakers, Baptists, Independents or Brownists, and Presbyterians. Nonconformity was significant in the city. Early Methodists however were sacrament-taking Anglicans, meeting as devotional groups outside normal church hours. The places where they

*81   6 Dowry Square, built c.1725*
*Here Dr. Thomas Beddoes, Reader in Chemistry at Oxford 1788-92, set up his 'Pneumatic Institution' to treat diseases by inhalation. Beddoes' assistant was Humphrey Davy, inventor of the miners' safety lamp. He experimented with nitrous oxide as a means of anaesthesia.*

John Wesley's Chapel, Horsefair Bristol.

met could not accommodate large numbers so Wesley bought a piece of land in the Horsefair and had a structure erected known as the New Room, the oldest Methodist church in the world. It was initially built as a place to expound the scriptures to the religious societies of Nicholas and Baldwin Streets, and their acquaintances. In 1784, at a house in Dighton Street, John Wesley ordained Thomas Coke, who sailed from Old Passage on the Severn to America with two helpers. Previously, in 1771, in the New Room, Francis Asbury had volunteered for missionary service in America, and when Coke arrived in America he ordained Asbury and they became the first bishops of the Methodist Episcopal Church.

An important group among the 20,000 Dissenters in 18th-century Bristol were the Quakers. Although their numbers were always small, well under a thousand in 1700, and just over 600 by the

**82** *(above left)* ***The New Room, The Horsefair, built 1739***
*The New Room was the first Methodist Church in the world. John Wesley spent nearly 1,500 nights there from 1739-90. In the centre of the photograph is a two-decker pulpit, in front of which is the conmmunion table used by Wesley. Upstairs are study bedrooms for the preachers, and a Common Room.*

**83** *(left)* ***John Wesley's statue, The Horsefair, erected in the 1790s***
*Wesley was a Fellow of Lincoln College, Oxford, and missionary to Georgia, 1735-8. He came to Bristol in 1739 at the invitation of George Whitefield. He ordained his own ministers in 1784 for the American Methodists, and thus broke with the Church of England.*

**84** *(above)* ***Thomas Goldney's House, 1723***
*The house was rebuilt for Goldney II, 1720-3, by George Tully. Goldney was the greatest shareholder in the privateering voyage of Captain Woodes Rogers, 1708-11, which captured a Spanish treasure galleon. The Georgian glazing bars have been removed from the 18th-century wing of the house.*

**85** *(above right)* ***Nehemiah Champion's House, Clifton Court, 1742***
*Now the Chesterfield Nursing Home, this house was built for Martha Goldney and Nehemiah Champion c.1742. The east side of the house is composed of black refuse ore, cast in square blocks. These came from Champion's brass foundry on St Augustine's Back.*

**86** *(right)* ***William Watts' Shot Tower, Redcliffe Hill, built 1782***
*Redcliffe Hill Shot Tower was one of the earliest brick-built houses in Bristol and the first shot tower in the world. It was demolished in 1969 for road widening. William Watts, a plumber, patented his new process in December 1782. He extended his house upwards, and sank a well below, to achieve a drop of 120 feet.*

end of the century, this small community played a remarkable part in the life of the city. William Penn had married Hannah Callowhill in 1696 at the Friars' Meeting House, Broadmead, before setting off for America. He took James Logan, another Quaker, with him to Pennsylvania where Logan eventually became Chief Justice and Governor. The Champions were involved in Bristol porcelain, the brass industry, shipping and trade, as well as building a dock. The Harfords were involved in ironworks and banking. Abraham Darby, of Cheese Lane, invented the coking of coal. George Tully was a Quaker architect. All Champion's partners in the extensive Warmley Copper works and the brass foundry on St Augustine's Back, Thomas Goldney, Thomas Crosby and Sampson Lloyd, were Quakers. The Franks family and the Rings were leading local potters and the Farleys printed local newspapers. Another Quaker, Joseph Fry, was a partner in a pottery firm, an apothecary, a partner in a type foundry, and involved in a Bristol soap business.

Although Thomas Speed had shipped white slaves, Thomas Goldney and Nehemiah and William Champion had been involved in privateering, and William Champion supplied Guinea pots, Guinea kettles, and Manillas for the Bristol slave trade, the increasing organisational efficiency of Quakers in the second half of the century is reflected in their leading role in the campaign against that horrific trade. This is in stark contrast to the activities of the Merchant Venturers who frequently petitioned the government for aid or protection of their Africa trade. Equally important in the 18th century were the Quaker contributions to education, prison reform, and to the Bristol Library Society, founded in 1772-3.

**87  King William III's statue, Queen Square**
*Michael Rysbrack's statue is widely believed to be the finest in Europe. It was erected in 1736. The rider lacks stirrups and is barefoot. When Redcliffe Way was carved diagonally across this beautiful square in the 1930s the railings were removed and the statue turned 45 degrees.*

**88 Warmley Brass Works, built 1761**
*William Champion's works manufactured Guinea pans, Guinea kettles, brass cannons and other items for the Africa Trade. An inventory of 1761 listed 22 copper furnaces, 15 brass furnaces, three rolling mills, five water battery mills with 12 hammers, and one spelter works with five furnaces.*

Queen Anne died in August 1714. Towards the end of her reign, and right up to the wild speculation of the South Sea stock in 1720, occurred one of the most colourful and extraordinary feats of seamanship in Bristol's maritime history. Captain Woodes Rogers, whose house was in Queen Square, was only the third person, after Francis Drake and Thomas Cavendish, to circumnavigate the world. He had not intended to do so when he set sail from Bristol on 1 August 1708 in two new ships, *Duke* (350 tons and 36 guns) and *Duchess* (260 tons and 26 guns). His intention was a privateering voyage to the river Plate, to round the Horn, and to try to capture one, or both, the annual Manilla-Acapulco Spanish treasure galleons and to journey back round the Horn with the prize. The voyage occurred during the War of Spanish Succession, 1702-13, and the *Duke* and *Duchess* had 'letters-of-marque' from the Admiralty Court authorising them, as armed merchantmen, to cruise against the enemy and to seize prizes. They took the mariner, Alexander Selkirk, on board, after they had rounded the Horn and were recuperating on the island of Juan Fernandez. He had been on

the island for four years and four months, having disembarked from the *Cinque Ports* saying it was full of holes from Toredo worms and would sink. He was right.

The *Duke* and *Duchess* had sustained damage in rounding the Magellan Straits and in the course of their various sea fights, so the return trip had to be across the Pacific and by way of the Cape of Good Hope. They captured one of the two Acapulco galleons and sailed the treasure ship back to this country. The Bristol backers of this extraordinary voyage, which was immortalised in Defoe's *Robinson Crusoe*, profited hugely from the captured treasure. John Romsey, town clerk, gave two magnificent candlesticks to the cathedral which can be seen on the altar of the Eastern Lady Chapel.

Besides the monument to Colston in Colston Avenue which we have discussed already, there is another famous statue, given by Sir W.H. Wills, of Edmund Burke, M.P. for Bristol 1774-80. At that time the city's trade was almost as much with mainland America as with the West Indies. Burke was unquestionably the most distinguished orator in the House of Commons. He was a professional politician and the six years he represented Bristol constitute only a short chapter in his career. Bristol, almost alone of any constituency in 1774, elected a member who was pro-American. It was in the merchants' interest to maintain friendly relations with America in order to avoid disruption of trade and cancellation of debts. Burke spoke most eloquently from the opposition benches but made little impact on the government's policy. He only visited Bristol twice in six years and could not offer attractive pickings of the fruits of patronage as Lord Clare had been able to do previously. He made no effort to create an electoral organisation to support him and would not work with his fellow Bristol MP Cruger. Burke was defeated in the 1780 elections.

His relationship with his constituency had been unhappy. The merchants had resented his support

**89   Edmund Burke's statue, Colston Avenue, 1894**
*Burke was one of Bristol's two MPs at the time of the War of
American Independence and he argued the case of the former colonies.
He was the most outstanding orator in the House of Commons. He
antagonised many Bristolians and lost his seat in 1780 because his
ideas were ahead of their time.*

for relaxing penalties for debtors. Bristolians had
disapproved of his endeavours to relieve the Irish
Catholics from an oppressive penal code, and to grant
them toleration. On the matter of Ireland's trade laws,
he had supported the Irish against the interests of
the Merchant Venturers who had tried to keep
Ireland as almost a foreign country commercially,
outside our Old Colonial System. He was ahead of
his time and paid the penalty. It was 100 years before
he found favour in Bristol and a statue was put up in
his honour, whereas Wesley's recognition did not take
so long. His statue is equestrian and was erected in
the yard outside the New Room soon after his death.

# VII

# Brunel's Bristol and Popular Discontents

IT IS NOT GIVEN to many people to have their names associated with a particular period in a city's history: Haussman's Paris, Chamberlain's Birmingham, Wren's London. Yet Angus Buchanan is surely right to say that Brunel 'made a greater contribution to the landscape of the Bristol area than any other single individual before or since'. There is the evidence of his splendid bridge over the gorge, the railway network radiating from Bristol, his original Temple Meads station still intact at its centre and, because of the improvements which he introduced, the Floating Harbour survives. His most famous ship now rests in the dry dock from which she was launched in 1843. Brunel has been described as an engineering polymath.

He arrived at Clifton to convalesce after a serious accident sustained in 1828 while helping his father as Assistant Engineer on the Thames Tunnel project. In 1829 he heard of the Merchant Venturers' scheme to build a bridge across Avon Gorge and submitted four possible designs in the competition. His involvement with this city lasted for the next twenty years but his offices remained in London, and he never made his home here. He was not a Bristolian, and had been born at Portsea, 9 April 1806. The competition brought him into contact with an influential group of Bristolians who became his life-long friends. These included shipbuilders such as William Patterson and Christopher Claxton, industrialists such as T.R. Guppy, and merchants such as Nicholas Roch. It was probably Roch who introduced him to the promoters of the Great Western Railway and also to the Board of the Bristol Docks Company.

An unenlightened and penny-pinching policy towards Bristol's docks had typified most of the 18th century. It was always the wrong time to do anything about increasing the berthing space, lessening congestion at the port, and improving turn-around time for ships. If trade was depressed it was argued that money invested would not be recoverable. If trade was flourishing then why invest in dock facilities instead of merchandise? Various schemes to improve the port were put forward from the 1760s which failed to be implemented due to wrong timing, the problems of silting, the need for a tidal bypass, and stagnant city sewage. The Rev. William Milton, vicar of Temple Church, put forward a plan in 1791 which provided for a dam and lock chamber in the bed of the Avon itself, a new bed for the river along the flat land to Totterdown, and a second cut to take excess flood water and to top up the harbour. His scheme was not adopted because it seemed too costly at a time when the trade of the port was rising again. A very similar scheme to Milton's, however, proposed in December 1802 by Jessop and White, was put into effect between 1804 and 1809, transforming two and a half miles of the old river into a 'floating dock' covering 76 acres of water. A dam and feeder canal at Netham Weir conveyed clean water to the floating harbour and facilitated navigation to Bath.

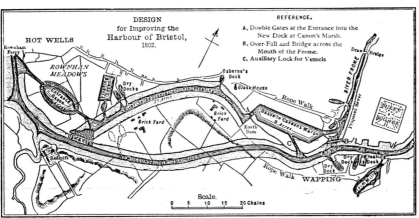

DESIGN
for Improving the
Harbour of Bristol,
1802.

REFERENCE.

A. Double Gates at the Entrance into the
   New Dock at Canon's Marsh.
B. Over-Fall and Bridge across the
   Mouth of the Frome.
C. Auxiliary Lock for Vessels

*Jessop's Plan for Floating the Harbour.*

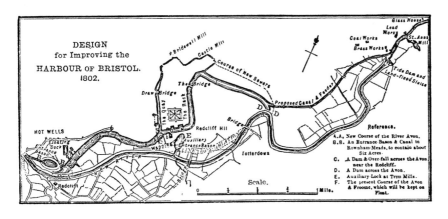

DESIGN
for Improving the
HARBOUR OF BRISTOL.
1802.

Reference.

A.A. New Course of the River Avon.
B.B. An Entrance Bason & Canal to
     Rownham-Meads, to contain about
     Six Acres.
C.   A Dam & Over-fall across the Avon
     near the Redcliff.
D.   A Dam across the Avon.
E.   Auxiliary Lock at Trim Mills.
F.   The present Course of the Avon
     & Froome, which will be kept on
     Float.

**90   Scott's Yard, called
'Nova Scotia', near the
overfall dam, April 1826, by
T.L.S. Rowbotham**
*This watercolour shows
shipbuilders at work on a hull,
with Clift House, formerly Red
Clift House, behind the timber
drying shed. The yard became
part of an island when the
Floating Harbour was created in
1804-9. The late Georgian
Nova Scotia Inn can be seen
on the left of the picture.*

**91   Jessop's Original and
Final Plans, 1802**
*In 1802 Jessop submitted plans
to convert the old bed of the Avon
into 76 acres of non-tidal harbour.
His original and final plans are
shown here. Cumberland Basin
was dug through Rownham
Meads in 1804-9.*

*92   Overfall dam of Cumberland Basin, c.1827*
*This watercolour by T.L.S. Rowbotham shows the overfall dam as it was before Brunel was consulted about the problems of silting and stagnant sewage in the Frome. He increased the flow of water by means of a culvert under the overfall dam.*

However, the Floating Harbour was prone to silt up. This problem was partly alleviated in 1828 by the construction of a culvert which redirected the stagnant sewer which was the river Frome and discharged it into the New Cut, which was swept by tides every 24 hours. But silting remained a problem and banks of mud were making parts of the harbour unusable. Brunel raised the height of the Netham Weir, thus directing more water from the Avon through the harbour, and he converted the Overfall Dam near Cumberland Basin by making a culvert underneath the dam, thus scouring silt into the tidal New Cut. It was henceforth called the Underfall.

Thomas Telford, first President of the Institute of Civil Engineers, was the judge of the competition for a bridge over the Avon Gorge in 1829. He had designed the Menai suspension bridge and this had convinced him (wrongly) that lateral wind resistance limited the possible span to 600 feet. Brunel's designs proposed spans of 870 feet to 916 feet and were rejected. Telford submitted his own scheme but that was rejected by the Merchant Venturers on the grounds that the proposed massive piers rising from the ground to shorten the span would be too expensive. A fresh competition was held in October 1830 which Brunel won with what he called his 'Egyptian thing', with a span of 630 feet and a large abutment from the foot of the Gorge on the Leigh Woods side.

It took far more money than had been originally contemplated, and the whole project was shelved for five years from 1831 to 1836. The two piers were completed in 1840, but for 20 years work stopped

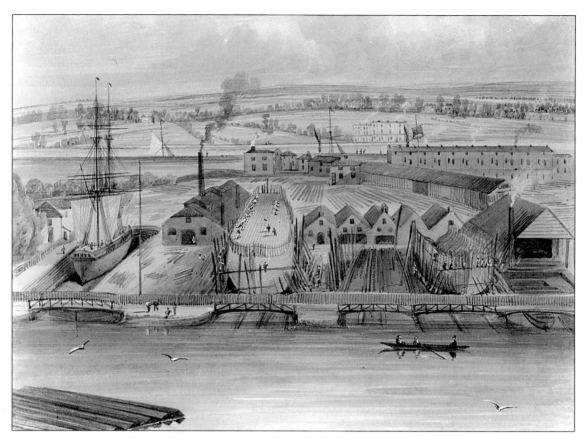

once more and the iron work, including the two double wrought-iron suspension chains, was sold to build the Royal Albert Bridge over the Tamar. It was only after Brunel's death in 1859 at the age of 53 that a new company was formed in 1861, specifically as a memorial to him, and work started again. This company were able to use the double chains from Brunel's Hungerford Bridge, then being dismantled to make room for Charing Cross Bridge, and the suspension bridge was formally opened on 8 December 1864. It has remained a thing of beauty and a source of wonder ever since.

Plans for a railway link between Bristol and London surfaced in the autumn of 1832. The new railway was promoted by the same group of Bristol merchants and businessmen who had supported the Clifton Bridge project and harbour improvements. They included T.R. Guppy, John Harford, C.P. Fripp,

John Cave, Henry Bush, and Nicholas Roch, who suggested Brunel as their engineer. Bristol became the hub of the broad-gauge system of 7 feet, rather than the narrow gauge of 4 feet 8½ inches, which was based on the width of the old Roman chariot wheels. The network was built largely with Bristol capital and Bristol enterprise and aimed to provide safe high-speed travel. It linked London and Bristol, pushed on into Devon and Cornwall, and fanned out into South Wales and the Midlands. Latimer, at the end of the 19th century, lamented 'the evil consequences of his (Brunel's) pet crochet, the "broad gauge" system, on the commerce of Bristol', and charged Brunel with being 'prone to seek for difficulties rather than to evade them, and utterly indifferent as to the outlay which his recklessness entailed upon his employers'. Such a view was not untypical at that time. Others, in his own time,

**93** (above left)  *Hillhouse's new dock at Mardyke, 1826, by T.L.S. Rowbotham*
This yard later came to be known as Albion Dockyard. These three docks were built on 10 acres at Mardyke and key workers lived in Sydney Row, shown on the right and behind. Also in the background, where there is a sail, is the New Cut. In the middle a large East India ship is being caulked. The Baltic Wharf site is to the right of the picture.

**94** (above)  *Entrance to Cumberland Basin, c.1840*
Jessop's north entrance lock is to the left and his south entrance lock is on the right. Brunel replaced this lock by one 262 ft. long and 52 ft. wide, to take larger ships. The SS Great Britain could not get through it without the stone facings being removed.

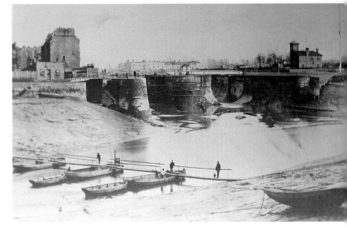

**95**  *Entrance to Cumberland Basin, c.1862*
Jessop's north entrance lock is to the left and Brunel's lock (built 1844-9) is to the right. Brunel's lock is now sealed by a concrete wall. His pedestrian swing bridge is clearly seen. Rownham ferry in the foreground was closed in 1933.

**BRIDGE UNDER CONSTRUCTION.**

A. SHOWING STAGING ON WHICH CHAINS WERE LAID. AUGUST 1863.

B.&C. THE ROADWAY UNDER CONSTRUCTION 1864 SHOWING GIRDERS, AND SADDLES ON TOP OF PIERS.

D. THE OPENING CEREMONY DEC. 8TH 1864. I.K.BRUNEL, ENGINEER.

**CLIFTON SUSPENSION BRIDGE**

**96   Clifton Suspension Bridge, c.1860**
*Brunel died four years before work to link the towers commenced in 1859. A new company was formed in 1861 which acquired the towers and approaches for £2,000. Chains were purchased from Hungerford Bridge, London, which Brunel had completed in 1843. Clifton Bridge opened on 8 December 1864.*

**97   Map of the City Docks**

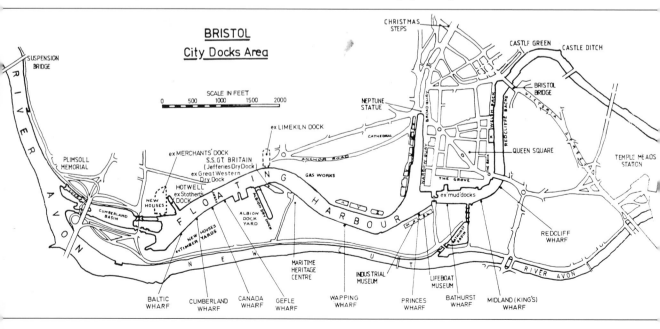

*98 (above)*  **Temple Meads in the 1860s**
*The Bristol and Exeter offices are in the distance and the wooden structure on the left, known as the 'cow shed', was the terminus of the Bristol and Exeter Railway line. The tracks in the foreground show both the Brunel 7 ft. broad gauge and the 4 ft. 8½ in. standard gauge.*

*99 (below)*  **Temple Meads, Brunel's Engine Shed, 1840s**
*This lithograph by John Bourne shows the cantilevered wooden roof with a 72 ft. centre span. The train shed is built on vaulting 15 feet above ground level. It is the most important terminus station from the early railway era.*

**100  Temple Meads and the Tramways Station, c.1913**
To the left a tram is emerging from the tram station. The fare board
says 1d. to Bristol Bridge, City and Tramways Centre. In the left
foreground is the taxi office, originally for horse-drawn taxis but,
from 1908, for petrol cars. Behind both buildings is Brunel's Old
Train Shed.

regarded him as a legend. He had the vision to see the GWR extending across the Atlantic by means of his three great ships.

Only two of his three ships were built in Bristol. The *Great Eastern*, built in London, was so large that there was never any possibility of her visiting the Avon. The first of the ships Brunel designed, the SS *Great Western*, was built by William Patterson in his yard which is now Prince's Wharf, near the Industrial Museum. It was an oak-hulled paddle steamer, strengthened with iron. It was 236 feet long, 59.6 feet broad, with four main masts carrying sails. It was launched on 19 July 1837 and had a remarkably successful career crossing the Atlantic. It convinced the sceptics that steam ships in ocean service could make the crossing without running out of coal. The speed, reliability and comfort of the *Great Western* was far superior to the American fast sailing boats of 300-500 tons which had dominated the North Atlantic up to 1837. Despite storms, icebergs, fogs and strong currents they did the journey in 18 days, but they were built for speed, not for passenger comfort. Emigrants leaving Europe had to squat or lie wherever they could, and to bring their own food and fresh water.

The SS *Great Britain* was originally to have been a sister ship, built of wood, powered by paddles. The arrival in Bristol of the *Rainbow*, an iron-hulled paddle ship, changed Brunel's mind. Similarly in May 1840 another experimental vessel, the *Archimedes*, visited Bristol. It was powered by a screw propeller designed by Sir Francis Petit Smith. Brunel chartered her for six months of experiments at the end of which, impressed by her manoeuvrability, he switched to a screw propeller for the *Great Britain*. His ship had an immensely strong iron hull with five bulkheads across with watertight doors, a balanced rudder for ease of turning, a screw propeller, hinged masts and wire rigging. The ship was 322 feet long and 51 feet broad. It had 113 two-berth cabins and 26 single cabins, a cargo capacity of 1,200 tons, and a crew of one

hundred and thirty. The engines produced 1,000
horse power, and the saloons were beautiful and hung
with pictures. It was the most advanced ship of its
day. With the help of the steam tug *Sampson*, the
*Great Britain* was finally heaved into the Avon on
12 December 1844, having spent 18 months trapped
in the Floating Harbour because the Cumberland
Basin locks were too narrow to let her through.

The great crowds that watched from the
surrounding hills that day were probably no different
in composition from those who were spectators at
some of Bristol's riots. Back in 1831, Brunel himself
was in Clifton on Saturday 29 October when the
Recorder of Bristol, Sir Charles Wetherell, a staunch
opponent of parliamentary reform, arrived in the
city for the Assizes. He was accompanied by a
detachment of Dragoons under Lt.-Col. Brereton.
He was met by a stone-throwing mob that later got
out of hand. Brunel and his friend Nicholas Roch
were sworn in as special constables and did what
they could at the Mansion House, and at the Bishop's
Palace, to salvage valuables and to discourage looters
as the buildings were put to the torch. Brunel actually
arrested a looter and marched him off to a magistrate.

**101   Brunel at the launch of the Great Eastern, 1858**
*In this photograph, possibly taken by Robert Howlett (1831-88),
Brunel stands with Earl Derby, who in 1858 was President of the
Board of Trade and Secretary of State for India, and with John Scott
Russell, F.R.S, in whose Napier Yard, Isle of Dogs, the Great Eastern
was built. They are watching the ship slide down the slipway.*

**102   SS Great Britain, 5 July 1970**
*The Great Britain is being towed up the Avon to Charles Hill's
Wapping Dock. It had been necessary to wait for a suitable tide
before undertaking the tricky manoeuvre of towing her round
Horseshoe Bend. On 19 July she was inched back into her original
dock.*

When, subsequently, Charles Pinney, Mayor of Bristol, was tried for neglect of duty, Brunel gave evidence.

The 1831 Reform Bill Riots in Bristol are notorious, but form the culmination of a series throughout the 18th and early 19th century. Hardly a decade went by in Bristol without some sort of major commotion involving food riots, riots against turnpikes, riots against Dissenters, Jews, and wage cuts. With no political rights and little means of exerting any political pressure, and a governing elite that treated the populace with utter contempt, the only way for the propertyless majority to address any grievance was to resort to the power of the crowd. For the urban labourers and the miners of Kingswood, the horrendous working conditions in the deeper mines, the longer hours in industrial workplaces, meant that life was lived at the margins. Protests were usually against change for the worse.

In the West Country the harvest of 1708 had been disastrous and the price of wheat was beyond the means of poor people. A terrible frost lasted without intermission from Christmas Eve till the middle of April. Large trees split and branches fell. Led by the Kingswood miners, and armed with cudgels, 400 people marched into the city on 21 May, demanding food. The city's poor who joined them had watched shipments of wheat being sent to France and Spain. The magistrates bought off serious trouble by promising that wheat would be sold on the following Monday at 6s. 8d. per bushel, then making sure the militia were ready and armed. In October 1714, the accession of the Hanoverians provided the spur for the miners to enter the city, to smash the windows of the Custom House in Queen Square, and to terrify Dissenters and Hanoverians. Jacobite sympathisers had primed the mob with drink. The area south of the river in Tucker Street suffered most damage. Those rioters who were caught and brought before three magistrates were dealt with amazingly leniently.

Roads around Bristol were notoriously bad, and one of the innovations of George I's reign was the establishment of turnpike tolls to improve the situation. Until this time every farmer paying £50 rent per annum was required to lend a wagon and horses for six days' use on the roads in each parish. Labourers and artisans had to give six days' work. The increase in coaching had greatly worsened these roads. In April 1727 a Private Bill received the Royal assent and set up a Turnpike Trust on the chief roads out of Bristol, for a distance of from 10 to 12 miles. Turnpike gates were installed to ensure collection of the necessary money for repairs. The tolls included a halfpenny for a packhorse laden with coals. The Kingswood miners destroyed the gates and burnt some of them. When re-erected they were thrown down by the miners, who prevented coal from entering the city. Some rioters wore women's clothes and high-crowned hats.

The riots spread and the following year the Kingswood miners marched to Chippenham and demolished the turnpike at Ford. They even threatened to pull down Blathwaite's house at Dyrham Park because he had attempted to defend the turnpikes. In 1734 every gate between Bristol and Gloucester had been destroyed. Further Acts were obtained leading to further riots in 1749 when a semblance of peace was only restored by calling out a regiment of Dragoons. Two ringleaders were hanged and five prisoners died in Newgate from smallpox.

In the spring of 1753 the poor were in great distress. In 1752 a cattle disease had decimated many herds in the area, and the 1752 harvest had been very bad. Hundreds of miners made their way to the Council House to protest that a cargo of wheat was about to be exported. A ship bound for Dublin with corn was plundered. Since the Council House windows had been smashed and many people injured, the militia were called out and citizens enrolled as special constables. Over several days 900 rioters attacked the Bridewell. The Dragoons arrived from

**103   Bristol Riots, 1831**
*These were the worst riots since the Gordon Riots in London 50 years before. Troops had to be used. The ostensible cause was the House of Lords' rejection of the Parliamentary Reform Bill. Many important civic buildings were destroyed.*

**104   Aerial view of Queen Square, The Grove and The Backs**
*Queen Square was built between 1699 and 1727. In the 1831 Riots all the houses on the north row and most of those on the west were burned down. At the bottom centre is the Bush Tea warehouse, built in two sections in 1832 and 1837 and now the Arnolfini Gallery.*

Gloucester and fired on the crowd. In various encounters four colliers were shot dead and nearly 50 wounded. More troops came from Worcester but the colliers continued to foment revolt in the area. They were particularly incensed at a wealthy woollen draper named John Brickdale who had shot a rioter. One of the coroners, Edward West, held an inquest and reached a verdict of wilful murder against John Brickdale, and others. West held more inquests on similar victims with similar verdicts. The government instituted proceedings in the Court of Kings Bench to quash these verdicts, and ordered a general pardon to Brickdale and others. Eight prisoners were condemned to two years in prison. The 1756 harvest was particularly dreadful and, since England was at that time at war with France, imports were few. Again the price of wheat rose beyond the pockets of the

poor people, and barges coming down the Severn and Wye with corn to relieve the dearth in Bristol, were plundered. Even a ship on her way down the Severn was stopped and plundered.

The worst riots of the century occurred in 1793 and concerned the tolls on Bristol Bridge, which was a bottleneck at that time. It carried the only road linking the north and the south of the city, and the next bridge was six miles upstream at Keynsham. Eighteenth-century traffic had so increased that there was usually a long wait to get across the bridge. The new Bristol Bridge, opened for traffic in 1769, had toll houses at the sides in the middle. Under the provisions of the Act of 1785, the trustees of the bridge were entitled to collect tolls until the money borrowed had been paid off, and a balance of £2,000 secured so that the interest on the sum would pay for lighting and maintenance. It had been announced by the solicitor of the trustees that tolls would cease in September 1793. This statement was never questioned but the bridge trustees announced the tolls would be collected for another 12 months and proceeded to ensure that they were. Riots ensued. Gates and toll boards were burnt. On 28 September the Herefordshire militia opened fire killing one man and wounding two or three. On the 30th the Riot Act was read three times and the militia ordered to fire again into the crowd. This time 11 were killed and 45 wounded, including a visitor and several onlookers. This ended the riots. Several leading citizens raised the money and paid three months rent to the trustees, so that tolls need not be charged, and the Corporation successfully prevented the trustees from being brought to court.

The Reform Bill Riots which Brunel witnessed led to the burning down of the Custom House and two sides of Queen Square, the Bishop's Palace, the toll houses and Gloucester County prison at Lawford's Gate, and some warehouses in Prince Street. They were ended by two troops of Light Dragoon Guards and one troop of 3rd Dragoon Guards finally charging across Queen Square with their sabres drawn, and clearing nearby streets. Twelve people were killed and 94 treated in the infirmary, but these were minimum figures. Some had died accidentally in the flames of the Mansion House and Custom House. Much property stolen from Queen Square houses was recovered in the Pithay, St Philip's and Marsh Street.

Bristolians had been incensed by reports that the Recorder of Bristol, Sir Charles Wetherell, who was not a Bristol MP, had asserted during debates in the House of Commons in 1831 that 'the citizens of the city were indifferent to reform'. He had made 180 interventions and speeches against the Bill, yet

he was an MP for a 'rotten' borough in Yorkshire, nominated by the Duke of Newcastle to represent his interests. Before the 1832 Act MPs could be nominated by wealthy patrons who owned many acres of land which had once sustained communities but were now unpopulated.

In Bristol, advocates of reform stirred up resentment against Sir Charles Wetherell's intemperate speeches and, inevitably, the populace saw an opportunity for trouble. Dr. Gray, the Bishop of Bristol, had incurred popular wrath in that, as a member of the House of Lords, he had consistently voted against the Reform Bill. Thus there were anti-clerical undertones as well as political aspects to the riots.

The 1831 riots had seen a wretched abdication of responsibility by the local authorities. There had been a period of control by the lawless elements, followed by the intervention of the military and the use of force. Bristol was profoundly shocked. Eighty-one rioters were convicted and four were hanged. The Reform Bill became an Act on 7 June 1832 and political power shifted to the urban middle classes. Among those who joined the rioters were some of the navvies working on the railway linking the mines of Coalpit Heath with the Harbour. This foreshadowed developments which were taking Bristol into the modern age.

# VIII

# *Shipbuilding, Sugar, Coal and Public Health*

THE RETURN TO PEACE after the War of American Independence (1776-83) had been a boost to business confidence. Cheap credit enabled Bristolians to engage in speculative canal schemes and to invest in the great building ventures in Clifton. However, more investment went to South Wales tin plate works, copper smelting and iron works than into Bristol's own hinterland industries. Not all was

well with Bristol's economy in the first half of the 19th century. Bristol's coalfields were proving increasingly difficult to mine. The seams were thin in the Kingswood area, between 1 ft. 3 in. and 2 ft., and in the Somerset coalfield between 10 in. and 2 ft. 4 in. Despite increased output from these mines the coalfields' share in UK coal output fell from 3.5 per cent in 1800 to less than 1 per cent of production

**105 (above)   Miners undercutting at Frog Lane Colliery, c.1905**
*The fuel needs of Bristol were met almost entirely from the Kingswood area of Gloucestershire. Handel Cossham (1824-90) owned the Kingswood Coal Company which raised one-fifth of the total in the coalfield which stretched from Iron Acton in the north to Pucklechurch in the south. The seams were thin.*

**106 (above right)   Pit bottom at Frog Lane, Coalpit Heath, c.1905**
*Hitchers with wooden tubs, each holding nine hundredweight of coal, loading into the cage. The colliery was sunk by the Coalpit Heath Collieries early in the 1850s. In 1947, 258 underground workers produced 3,500 tons each month. The pit was closed in 1949.*

**107 (right)   The cage at pit bottom, Frog Lane, Coalpit Heath, c.1905**
*By 1905 coal and men were raised by a horizontal winding engine which could raise 400 tons of coal in 10 hours in a two-deck cage as illustrated. Water was removed at a rate of 503,000 gallons every 10 hours.*

**108   South Liberty Colliery, c.1920s**
*This was one of several pits in the Bedminster area owned by Ashton Vale Iron Works. It was part of the Somerset coalfield which stretched from Clutton to Dunkerton, and from Pensford to Kilmersdon, six miles by eight miles. South Liberty, Bedminster, closed in 1925.*

**109   Miner using tugger and chain, Easton Colliery, 1910**
*Easton Colliery opened in 1881 and closed in 1911. The seams were very thin, just 1 ft. 3 in. to 2ft. Easton, with Speedwell and Whitehall pits, was owned by the Kingswood Coal Company. Whitehall was the largest pit, and in 1890 employed 1,000 men.*

by 1850. Industry tended to shift nearer the major coalfields of South Wales, South Lancashire and the north-east.

Mendip lead mines produced metal suitable for bullets and shot but not for plumbing and roof sheeting so the industry was in decline. Also in decline were the copper, brass, glass and gunpowder industries since competition had increased from the lower cost areas of the north of England. Bristol's potteries which had flourished at Temple Back and Redcliffe in the 18th and early 19th centuries, were too small to compete with the economies of scale possible in Staffordshire.

The slave trade was abolished within the British Empire in 1807, and all slaves were emancipated in 1833 at a cost of £20 million compensation to former owners, yet under the protective duties, payable under the Old Colonial System, merchants remained active. At the close of the 18th century the West India trade alone was worth twice as much

to Bristol as all her other overseas trade combined. Commerce with the Caribbean had saved most of the merchant community during the embargoes, shipping losses and bad debts which occurred during the war with the American colonies. However, of the twenty or so sugar refineries in Bristol from 1724 to 1780, seven closed during the 1780s owing to shortages in the supply of raw sugar. After the Napoleonic War profits in sugar sales were squeezed as world supplies increased and import duties rose. The number of sugar refineries in Bristol fell from 14 in 1818 to six in 1838, and by 1852 only two were left. The last one closed in 1908. This decline came about, despite Conrad Finzel's wide use of steam power and centrifugal machines, because of international competition and the growth of the sugar beet industry. After Peel's Free Trade measures in the 1840s a rapid decline in Bristol's trade with the West Indies occurred.

For many historians this apparent decline in

Bristol's competitive position is linked to the complacency of the West India merchant elite in Bristol. The leading families of Elton, Bright, Ames, Miles, Prothero, Pinney, Daniel and Hobhouse intermarried and avoided seriously competing with each other. Much of their capital was tied up in plantations and Caribbean mortgages and was not easy to repatriate. They were heavily represented on Bristol's old Corporation before 1835. The old Corporation contained a large number of aged and very conservative members. For instance, Brickdale was a councillor for 57 years, and his old rival Cruger for 61 years. Bernard Alford has widened the indictment by asserting that the whole commercial spirit of Bristol by the 1830s was stagnant. Bristol's businessmen were making poor entrepreneurial decisions, and he says, they did not match the vigour, marketing skills or enterprise of Glaswegians or Liverpudlians. They had become an inbred oligarchy. His review of 72 principal towns in the United Kingdom shows Bristol to have fallen from second to tenth position in population between 1801 and 1901. The signs of Bristol's relative economic decline can be seen in the fortunes of the port.

After the new harbour was opened in 1810 a multitude of dues, administered by the Corporation and the Society of Merchant Venturers, gradually strangled the port's commerce. A paper presented by the Bristol Chamber of Commerce in 1823 to unite action against these dues showed that the charges on 44 selected imports would be £515,608 at Bristol, £231,800 at Liverpool, £210,098 at London, and £147,587 at Hull. Add these prohibitive charges to congestion in the port, an up-river site, and the second highest tidal range in the world, and Bristol's problems are not surprising. So serious was the crisis over the high dues, and so much trade was being lost, that a Free Port Association was formed and played a key role in saving the port from ruin. The Corporation asked Parliament to permit an earlier transfer of the docks to the city than was

**110  Free Port Movement Demonstration, 1848**
*S. G. Tovey's painting of this great demonstration of 15 November 1848 shows civic dignitaries, trade associations, and the general public passing over the drawbridge. They were celebrating the freeing of the port of Bristol from the control of the Docks Company and the chance of lower charges and dues.*

envisioned in the Dock Company's Act. This was achieved in 1848 by Act of Parliament. The success of the Free Port movement was celebrated by a great public demonstration on 15 November 1848. However, the opening of deep water docks did not occur at Avonmouth until 1877 and Portishead in 1879. These were brought into municipal ownership in 1884, and were linked to the city by rail.

On the other hand, Charles Harvey and Jon Press have argued that Bristol in the 19th century was more than just a decaying maritime centre, with 'the majority of surviving industries … tied to the methods of the workshop rather than the factory'. They point out that the population grew to 330,000 by 1901, 'and with municipal parks, well-lit streets, class-differentiated suburbs, local newspapers, and an efficient transport network, it could claim to be a truly modern city'. They emphasise the long-term resilience of a number of industries in and around Bristol: Fry's were employing 4,600 people in 1908,

**111    Chocolate Factory of J.S. Fry and Sons, Pithay, 1924**
*In 1810 29 empty old houses in the Pithay were for sale. Frys acquired much of the Pithay to extend their factory in 1897. The company had started in Union St in 1793, the workforce growing from 11 to 350 by 1866 and to 4,600 by 1908.*

in eight factories, Wills' were employing 3,000 people when they merged in 1901 to form Imperial Tobacco; Packer's became Bristol's second largest chocolate firm when they moved to Eastville in 1900.

Shipbuilding and repairing continued to be an important part of Bristol's economy in the 19th century. Substantial yards were opened, of which Hillhouse's Chatham Yard (renamed Albion in 1848) was the largest. Bristol's shipbuilders adapted from oak to iron and later to steel for their hulls. The building of two of Brunel's advanced ships in Bristol yards suggests a willingness to innovate and experiment with new technologies. But the size of ship that could be constructed was limited by the twists and turns of the river, and the late 19th century witnessed the closure of many yards due to the cheaper cost of steel in the north of England. The Albion yard, which had been taken over by Charles Hill and Sons in 1848, continued to build ships up to 3,600 tons, floating cranes, dredgers, barges, and lock gates up to 1976. It finally closed in 1977 having built 477 ships including many frigates and corvettes during the Second World War. At the peak of pro-

**112** *(left)*   **Welsh Back, 1862**
*Goods cluttering the waterfront are largely unprotected. Ashmead's 1828 map shows seven very small sheds at the lower end of the Back. These were primitive open structures with tiled roofs carried on timber posts.*

**113** *(below)*   **St Augustine's Parade, c.1865**
*An Irish boat lies alongside the Dublin Shed. The small tower in the foreground once carried signals to shipping as to when it was clear to leave the harbour. Outside St Mary-on-the-Quay is a huge pile of sugar beet. Behind the church is the chimney of a sugar house.*

duction in 1945 Charles Hill and Sons were employing 1,350 men and 60 women.

Other long-term industries which continued to prosper included soap making. By the 1870s Christopher Thomas and Brothers was producing 8 per cent of the UK total, and had diversified into margarine manufacture, but it was taken over in 1910 by Lever Brothers, and production finally ceased in 1950. Glass making was another long-established industry. Hooper's glasshouse in St Philip's, conveniently close to the river, was taken over in 1824 by William and Thomas Powell. The firm was known as Cookson's and Powell's until 1828. In 1853 Powell's merged with Richard Ricketts and Company, and introduced gas-regenerating furnaces.

**114   The Old Drawbridge, St Augustine's Parade, 1880**
*There was a bascule bridge here in 1755. This was followed in 1827 by a drawbridge, with an 18 ft. carriageway. In 1868 this was replaced by another drawbridge weighing 130 tons. A fixed bridge was built at this point and opened on 6 May 1893. The water from here back to Stone Bridge was covered over.*

Powell and Ricketts of Avon Street stayed in business until 1923.

It was 1838 before cotton was produced in quantity in Bristol. The Great Western Cotton works, by the Feeder canal at Barton Hill, used steam, and employed 1,500 workers throughout the 19th century, making calico and cotton goods. It survived until 1925. Growing up alongside these industries were newer ones such as Bristol Gas Light company,

1817, and Bristol and Clifton Oil company, 1823, which merged in 1853. Gas holders were constructed and the Stapleton Road gasworks began production in the 1880s on a 40-acre site at Eastville. By 1930 more than 90 per cent of cooking in Bristol relied on gas, and gas continued to be produced there until the 1970s. Similarly, the Bristol Waterworks was established in 1846, and Bristol Tramways in 1874. A municipally owned electricity supply began in the early 1890s with power stations at Temple Back (1891), the Avonbank alongside the Feeder (1902), and Portishead (1926-9). E.S. and A. Robinson began manufacturing wrapping paper in Redcliffe Street

in 1844. It expanded into paper sacks and stationery and by 1914 was employing over 2,500 people. Boot and shoe manufacturers were traditionally small concerns, but a few such as Derham Brothers of Kingswood employed 1,500 in 1883.

Metal working and heavy engineering, waggon and carriage works, and steam locomotive manufacture were among the newer industries emerging as ship building, and brass and copper works declined. In these areas Bristol built up an international reputation. Lysaght's employed 400 in Bristol. The Bristol Waggon and Carriage works, formed in 1866 at Lawrence Hill, employed 900

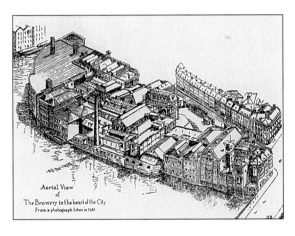

*115 (above)* **Overview of George's Brewery, Counterslip, 1932**
*William George of Worcester, distiller, occupied premises in Baldwin Street in 1736. Philip George bought a Porter Brewery in Bath Street in 1788. Between 1911 and 1923 George's acquired five firms, 305 licensed properties, and a total of 850 pubs. They bought the Counterslip site in 1924.*

*116 (above right)* **The Exchange Clock has two minute hands**
*On 30 June 1841, when Brunel's first through train arrived from London, Bristol was nearly 11 minutes behind Greenwich Mean or Railway Time. This clock showed both local and railway times. After September 1852 Bristol adopted G.M.T., anticipating Parliament by 30 years.*

*117 (right)* **The open river Frome and Stone Bridge, 1885**
*The photo shows a glimpse through to Rupert Street. In the centre is the figurehead from the SS Demerara which broke her back in the Avon in 1851 on her maiden voyage. In 1893 this scene was lost when the Frome was culverted.*

men. Douglas Engineering of Kingswood manufactured bootmaking machinery in 1882, motorcycles in 1907, motor cars in 1913 and, in the 1930s, aero engines. Roberts and Daines, William Butler and Company, Strachan and Henshaw, Bristol Tramways and Carriage Company, Thrissell Engineering, to name a few, were all new companies founded in the 19th century, providing technologically advanced products, and work for Bristol's growing population.

The 19th century had seen Bristol's population increase from 40,800 in the census of 1801 to 328,800 in that of 1901, and these figures are at the root of the problems concerning clean water, sewage disposal, and slum housing. Victorian Bristol was a combination of elegance and squalor. It rejoiced in splendid scenery, a mild climate, favourable land

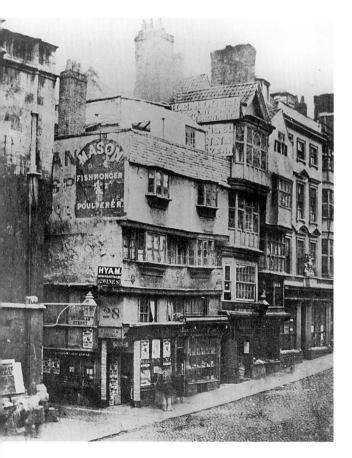

**118** (above)   *St Augustine's Parade at junction with Colston Street, c.1850*
*This is an exceptionally early photograph. The horse and men are sharp and clear considering the lengthy exposure that would have been needed. The row of shops to the left is recognisable but the rest has been completely transformed.*

**119** (left)   *High Street, 1857*
*Nicholas Street is on the immediate left. A number of 16th-century buildings are on the left-hand side of the cobbled street. No. 28 is a chop shop, the Druid's Arms, selling mutton chops at four for 6d. Affixed to the building is a firemark. Nicholas Street was rebuilt 1860-6.*

**120** (right)   *Original Corn Exchange, Narrow Quay, 1840s*
*This Corn Exchange was demolished in 1849. It had been used as the corn market for grain brought up the river. Another market in Wine Street dealt with grain transported by land. To the left, on the quay, is a column with a sundial, which stood there for 200 years until the Dublin Shed was built in 1862.*

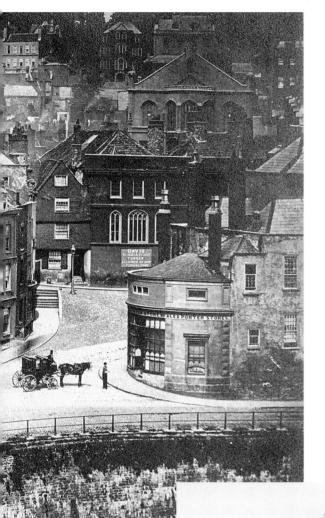

drainage, and it stands on carboniferous limestone and several sandstones which are favourable to water retention and to springs and wells. Yet Sir Henry De La Beche and Dr. Lyon Playfair reported in 1845 that Bristol was the third most unhealthy city in the country. Only the industrial centres of Liverpool and Manchester had higher general mortality rates than Bristol. Yet Bristol was regarded more as a seaport city than as a manufacturing town.

G. T. Clark, in his Report to the General Board of Health (1850) on the sewage, drainage and supply of water in Bristol, said that the houses of the labouring poor were constructed without any regard to sanitary requirements. 73,836 labourers' and artisans' families fitted into 12,306 houses whose rated rental did not exceed £10 per annum. The dock improvements of 1804-9 effectively cut off the old city from the cleansing action of the Avon tides. Dams, entrance basins and locks, meant that the river Frome became virtually stagnant. The commissioners of paving, cleansing and lighting, appointed by the Corporation in 1806, had to take the Dock Company to the Court of King's Bench in 1826 to force them to discharge the putrid, untreated sewage into the

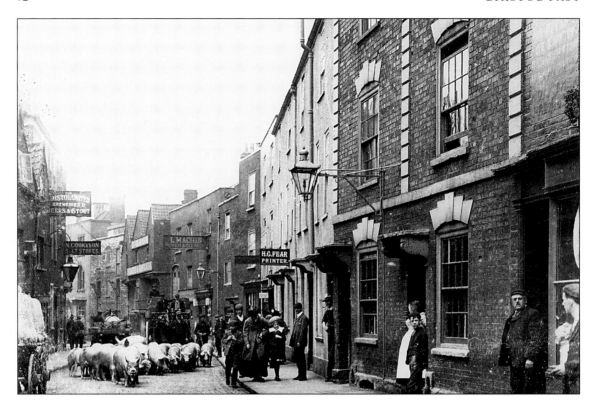

New Cut rather than the Frome. Nevertheless the districts of Temple and Redcliffe still continued to discharge 20,000 tons of foetid matter per annum into the Floating Harbour.

Even in Clifton the majority of the substantial houses drained into a cesspit. Victoria Square was an exception worth mentioning because it belonged to the Society of Merchant Venturers and they insisted on proper sewers for their development. They created open gardens, spacious footpaths, and forced Samuel Hemming, the owner of Lansdown Parade, to comply with their plans and to fill in Lansdown's cesspit. Upper Clifton largely drained down the hill to Hotwells.

Bedminster was practically undrained, as was St Philip's. Privies for the poorer classes were totally deficient for their needs, sometimes with fewer than three privies to 14 houses. These were almost invariably filthy and in bad repair. In 1850 in Hotwells there were 56 courts, only four of which were

*121 (above)*   ***Market Day, Broadweir, in the 1900s***
*Ellbroad Street (between Redcross Street and Broadweir) on market day. This street has not entirely disappeared in the building of Broadmead Shopping Centre. Street lighting is by gas.*

*122 (above right)*   ***St Augustine's Bridge, c.1892***
*Horses are in use everywhere, pulling trams and carts, although there is one handcart. To the left is St Augustine the Less, and the ornate transit shed on Deans Wharf. It is said the unusual architecture is due to its proximity to the approach to Clifton.*

*123 (right)*   ***Baldwin Street, c.1896***
*In 1891 the Council recommended 90 arc lights of 1,000 candle power each should be erected in the central streets. A new power station was built at Temple Back. By 1893 Bristol Bridge and the neighbouring thoroughfares were lit by electricity. Having the road up is nothing new in Baldwin Street evidently.*

supplied by a water company. Of 995 houses in streets in Hotwells, only 220 were supplied by a water company.

Spring conduits were available at Redcliffe, St John's, Temple, St Thomas', Quay Pipe and All Saints. Wells were available in many parts of the city but, according to Beche and Playfair, in many localities

cesspool fluids found their way into wells. Bristol's high death-rate statistics were a result of the ravages of the water-borne diseases of typhoid, cholera and dysentry. Yet within just over twenty years *The Times* observed (18 October 1869) that Bristol had been transformed 'from nearly the most unhealthy to be the most healthy town in Britain'. This remarkable transformation was manifest in the reduction in the general mortality rate from 28 per thousand in 1850 to 22 per thousand in 1869.

Those responsible for working this change were the Sanitary Committee of the Local Board of Health, the Bristol Waterworks Company, Dr. William Budd, physician to the Bristol Royal Infirmary, and David Davies, the city's first Medical Officer of Health. Two factors in particular drove the transformation: the first Public Health Act of 1848 and the cholera epidemic of 1849. Over the next 15 years a massive programme of mains drainage was carried out. The Sanitary Committee used its powers

**124   Wine Street, c.1900**
*Christ Church is in the centre distance. Horse-drawn vehicles seem
to be the only means of locomotion. Caps appear to be standard
wear for men. Verrier and Co., selling flannel, blankets and curtains
are certainly insistent.*

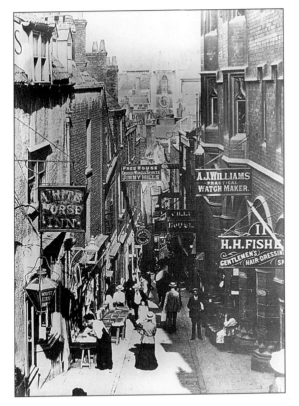

under the Nuisances Removals Act, 1855 to take proceedings against owners of filthy privies, requiring them to be connected with the mains sewers. By the late 1850s the main city streets were cleansed daily and the courts and alleys were provided with iron refuse bins.

The water company decided to draw its water supplies from springs in the Mendips and constructed reservoirs which were able to supply Bristol with four million gallons of water daily. It took much longer to connect up the homes of the labouring poor, but this was accomplished by 1866. It did not solve all public health problems overnight, however. Overcrowding and slums set their own limits on what could be achieved. Tuberculosis was the single most virulent killing disease in mid-Victorian England, and the bacillus was not identified until 1882, while penicillin was not available till the 1940s. However, pure water supply was the answer to those other killers, typhoid and cholera. Thanks to the independent research of Dr. William Budd, which mirrored Dr. John Snow's work in London, it was shown that these diseases originated from organisms carried in polluted water, and could be prevented by ensuring a pure water supply and strict hygiene for patients and their surroundings.

A typhus epidemic swept the poorer parts of the city in the autumn and winter of 1864 and finally forced the Sanitary Committee, under the Public Health Act of 1848, to appoint a Medical Officer of Health, Dr. David Davies. The organisation that he set up to deal with the epidemic was soon extended

**125  Christmas Steps, leading to St John on the Wall, c.1900**
*Bookstalls, straw boaters and huge lamps outside licensed premises recall the age just before the First World War. Formerly Knifesmith Street, this was the scene of bloody fighting during the Civil War.*

**126  High Street, 1908**
*The street marks the birthplace of the city as a place of traders, by the bridge across the river. There is a singular absence of wheeled traffic. St Nicholas on the immediate left has a number of top-hatted gentlemen outside on the pavement. St Nicholas Street was rebuilt in 1860-6.*

**127** (above)  **Regent Street, Clifton Village, c.1900**
*The road to the left is Merchants' Road, which was a hauling way for Carter's Brewery and was bought by the merchants from Francis Adams. On the corner is the large department store of Cordeux and Sons which opened in 1863. Upstairs 400 staff made clothes to order.*

**128** (below)  **Clifton Grand Spa Hydro, 1909**
*A final attempt to re-establish the Hotwell Spa was made at the end of the 19th century. In 1890 Sir George Newnes commenced to link the Hotwell Road Tramway Terminal with Sion Hill, Clifton, by means of a cliff railway. The hotel was opened in 1898 and the Pump Room beside it in 1894. The Pump Room became a cinema in 1920.*

to the whole city. Overcrowding remained a problem. At the same time that people were migrating out of the old city to suburbs such as St George, Bedminster and Stapleton, Bristol's population between 1861 and 1871 increased by almost a quarter (22.3 per cent), which brought its own problems. Nevertheless, in the space of twenty years public health had been spectacularly improved.

As Bristol's population climbed from 40,800 in 1801 to 328,800 in the census of 1901, the Anglican Church rose to the challenge and built many new churches. The 18th century had seen little building of churches in Bristol and four had become ruinous. To change this situation had not been easy because a large part of an incumbent's income came from fees for weddings and funerals. To reduce the number of parishioners would interfere with their financial and legal rights and the incumbents therefore opposed new churches. Another problem arose from pew rents. Renting out pews was an obvious way to maintain new churches and to provide an income where there were no endowments. Pew owners treated them as freehold property, however, and put them up for sale, thus depriving the church of the income they would have provided. However, Bishop

James Monk, of the joint sees of Bristol and Gloucester from 1836, gave a strong lead and, by 1847, 11 new churches were in the course of being built, some of them in desperately poor neighbourhoods. Further difficulties arose with the growth of parties in the Church of England, such as Tractarians, Anglo-Catholics and Evangelicals. Until 1898 patronage over the appointment to church livings was regarded in English law as a property right and could be bought and sold. Church party interests saw this as a way of extending their influence.

Bishop Charles John Ellicott succeeded Monk as Bishop of Bristol and Gloucester in 1863 and he also gave a strong lead. In 1868 the Bristol Church Aid Society was founded. The Society encouraged wealthier churches to support curates in poorer parishes. Ellicott was strongly supported by the Headmaster of Clifton, Dr. John Percival, in cooperation with the teaching staff. By the close of the century the city had expanded to include St George and Stapleton and the Anglican church had risen to the challenge of the vastly increased population by building 47 new churches.

IX

# *Avonmouth, Aeroplanes and the Blitz*

THE PORT OF BRISTOL was in the wrong place. Even the Romans, who needed an embarkation terminal for their assault on South Wales, picked a spot much nearer to the mouth of the Avon at Sea Mills, rather than seven miles up such a tidal river. In 1712 there was a short-lived attempt to build a dock there again. Vested interests at Pill also prevented the use of steam tugs, in place of oarsmen, to get ships up and down the river. The Clyde had steam tugs in 1803, and the Mersey, Tyne and Thames followed shortly after. It was 1836 before Bristol's first steam tug, the *Fury*, began to operate. Even then, 30 oarsmen boarded the tug at gunpoint one night and tried to scuttle it. Correspondents argued in the press as early as 1823 (*Bristol Journal*, 1 February), for a landing place to be built at Avonmouth. Most Bristolians could not accept that their newly built Floating Harbour could already be obsolete.

Brunel had the vision to see his rail link with London had tremendous implications for Bristol. In 1836 the Great Western Steamship Company was founded, and the first of Brunel's great transatlantic liners was launched in 1837. She completed the trip to New York in 14 days 16 hours, and the trip back in 12 days 14 hours. This was just what Bristol needed to restore her prestige as a seaport city, but the *Great*

*Western* had to anchor off Avonmouth and to transfer passengers and cargo by small boats. The Dock Company refused to consider Brunel's proposals for a pier at Portishead and soon the ship stopped coming to Bristol altogether. The *Great Britain*, built later, was three times the size of the *Great Western* and had great problems in getting through the locks into the river. It had no choice afterwards but to sail from Liverpool.

On 10 November 1851 the *Demerara*, a new paddle steamer of 3,000 tons, left Patterson's yard towed by a tug, went through the Cumberland Basin, and swung broadside across the river below Sea Walls, and as the tide ebbed she settled and twisted. It was a warning to all owners of big ships that a port seven miles up a narrow river was a hazard. The *Kron Prinz* on 1 April 1874 failed to get round Horseshoe Bend below Sea Mills, and she lay on her side for three weeks spilling 7,000 quarters of barley up and down the river, until she was finally shifted. This strengthened the case for docks at the mouth of the river.

In 1861 the Port Railway and Pier Company sought parliamentary approval for powers to build a pier at Avonmouth, linked by a railway line to Hotwells, but the City Corporation opposed the measure. The company succeeded in 1862 and two years later the pier and railway were opened. A rival company, the Bristol and Portishead Pier and Railway Company, opened their alternative line in 1868. The next step was to secure the construction of large

**129   Cumberland Basin, c.1879**
*It is high tide and ships are passing into the harbour through the lock gates. No. 29 bonded warehouse has not yet been built. The Dock Master's house (1858) and Waterford Shed (1879) are visible on the south side of the basin, but the Cork Shed was not built until 1880.*

*130 (above)* **Mary Ann Peters, 1857**
*This Bristol barque of 610 tons, which regularly carried passengers to Quebec from Bristol, became stranded on the mud at Rownham Ferry, 14 March 1857. It was not refloated until 31 March.*

*131 (above right)* **Wreck of Kron Prinz, 1874**
*On 1 April 1874 the Kron Prinz, a steamer from Germany loaded with barley, struck the bank near Horseshoe Point and was wrecked. Her masts and funnels were removed and she was refloated on 20 April, and repaired in Albion Dock.*

*132 (right)* **Timber Wharves on the South Bank, 1931**
*Baltic Wharf is now a housing development. Vessels tied up beside platforms mounted on barges. The wharves were named Onega, Canada, Cumberland, and Gefle (or Garle, after the timber exporting port in Sweden).*

modern docks. The first turf of Avonmouth Dock was cut on 26 August 1868 and the dock was opened on 24 February 1877. It had been built by a private company. Portishead had been rejected as the site for dock extension after a very bitter struggle between competing parties. Nevertheless, in 1879, a rival dock was built at Portishead and also linked to the city by railway.

In the years that followed, the original area of Avonmouth dock, 16 acres, proved inadequate and an arm was constructed, increasing the area to 19 acres. Warehouses and granaries were constructed with 29 steam and hydraulic cranes. These facilities meant that Elders and Fyffes, for example, could supply Bristol with 30,000 to 50,000 bunches of bananas each week. Apples arrived from New Zealand and Australia. The import of grain, cotton seed and linseed was stimulated by the building of mills in close proximity to the docks. Great quantities of petroleum were also handled at Avonmouth after the construction of storage tanks 90 feet in diameter, each with a capacity of 1,680,000 gallons.

Work started in 1902 on the Royal Edward Dock which was opened on 9 July 1908. This new basin had an entrance lock 875 feet long and 100 feet wide, and had a dry dock of the same length. Its water area covered 25 acres and a new railhead served a vast hinterland. Long piers 900 feet and 1,200 feet long stretched out to the Channel, enabling liners to land passengers and baggage directly onto a train alongside. Further extensions to the Royal Edward Dock were made later. On 1 September 1884 the Port of Bristol had purchased both Avonmouth and Portishead docks, thus ensuring Bristol's future as a seaport city destined to play an important part in two world wars. These new docks were vital to one aspect of her future development.

Another indication of Bristol's growth came in the early months of 1910 when Sir George White announced the formation of the British and Colonial Aeroplane Company. George White must surely stand with Edward Colston as one of the most

**133   Albion Dry Dock, c.1938**
*Albion began life as New Dockyard, owned by Hillhouse and Sons. In 1848 the company became Charles Hill and the dock was renamed Albion. Albion was 540 feet long and the largest dock in the harbour.*

*134   Traffic jam, Baldwin Street, 1920s*
*An amazing assortment of electric trams, petrol buses, horse and carts, motor cars and lorries. Perhaps workmen are digging up the road once more further along.*

significant figures in the city's history. He was born in Kingsdown in 1854, the second son of Henry White, painter and decorator. At the age of 15 George White became a junior clerk with a firm of solicitors, Stanley and Wasbrough. In 1870, through his work on Enabling Bills, he became familiar with tramway promotion. Subsequently he was involved in railways, docks, shipping, the city's Stock Exchange, and eventually in founding an aeroplane company. White was made company secretary of the Bristol Tramways Company. The tramway system started with horse-drawn vehicles in 1875. He left the law firm and became a member of the Bristol Stock Exchange in 1876, setting up his own firm, George White and Company. His contacts in the Western Wagon Company, of which Henry Gardner was vice-

chairman, enabled him to secure money advances to fund his dealings in stocks and shares which became the centre of his business world.

By 1910 Sir George headed a large business which had electrified trams not only in Bristol but in several other cities, and which manufactured motor omnibuses and taxis. His factory in South Bristol could produce 300 buses, lorries and taxis a year. His holding company operated 17 distinct tramway services, 15 bus services, and owned a fleet of 169 tramcars, 44 buses, 29 charabancs and 124 taxis. It had a workforce of over 2,000 and was one

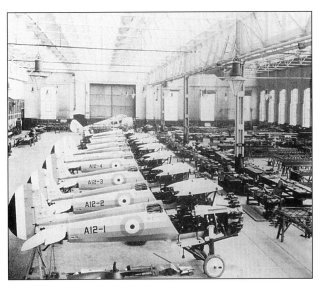

*135 (above)* **British and Colonial Aeroplane Company's works at Filton, 1912**
*A Bristol biplane of 1910 usually called a 'Boxkite' is flying overhead. The first flight, made in June 1910 by the French pilot Edmond, had been a success and more Boxkites were constructed at Filton.*

*136 (top right)*
**Bristol 'Bulldog' production line, Filton, 1929**
*This was the RAF's principal front-line fighter in the early 1930s.*

*137 (above right)*
**Lord Rothermere's plane, Bristol Type 143, 1935**
*This plane was called 'Britain First', and built as a private plane for the owner of the* Daily Mail. *It proved much faster than outmoded bi-planes then being built for the RAF, and it was clear that it would make an effective light bomber. Its design influenced the Mark 1 Blenheim which went into service with the RAF in 1937.*

of the biggest employers in Bristol. George White met Bleriot and some of his colleagues in 1909. Drawing on suitable labour from the Tramways Company's works at Brislington, and funding from members of his own family, he and his brother Samuel set up the British and Colonial Aeroplane Company at Filton, an area which was unusually fog free. There he made British adaptions of French aircraft, with French engines. The company also set up flying schools, and by August 1914 nearly half the 650 qualified pilots in the country had been trained by British and Colonial. By the time war came White was employing 400 workers at Filton, and had the capacity to make a plane a day.

Bristol's war history is largely the work of the port, and both before and after White's unexpected

**138   Wills ladies in the 'Stripping Room', 1919**
*W.D. and H.O. Wills moved to East Street, Bedminster in 1886. Wills ladies had to provide suitable Sunday School references and pass a sewing test for dexterity. They had to sign indentures that 'they would not contract Matrimony within the said term, or play at Cards or Dice'. Wills had a workforce of 3,000.*

death in 1916, the expansion of his aircraft company. The Bristol Fighter began to be produced in volume before White's death on 22 November 1916, and more than 3,500 were eventually constructed. By the end of the First World War the Bristol Aeroplane Company (as it was called from 31 December 1919) employed 8,000 workers. Glyn Stone has pointed out that the name change was in order to avoid the punitive effects of the Excess Profits Duty. He states that existing businesses which had discontinued, and had their assets transferred to a new company, paid less. Wartime profits were thus retained and the company's stability secured.

The engines division at Patchway proved the company's salvation in the interwar years. By taking over the Cosmos Engineering Company in Fishponds, after the War, the BAC acquired Roy Fedden, its chief engineer, and his team of engine designers, thus becoming the UK's leading aero-engine manufacturer as well as airframe constructor. The Jupiter engine powered the Bristol Bulldog, created in 1927, which became the RAF's standard fighter for some years, and was sold to the air forces of eight other nations. As rearmament proceeded the workforce grew and by 1938 reached 14,000. Filton and Patchway became important industrial areas. The Bristol Blenheim, powered by Mercury engines made in Bristol, was the first British aircraft in action in 1939. The Second World War saw the 'dispersal' of some of BAC's eventual 52,000 employees to Banwell, Weston-super-Mare and

**139 (above)    Welsh Back and Redcliffe Back, c.1912**
*Many of the buildings on the right bank were destroyed in the
Blitz. The barges, middle left, are tied up alongside Hide Shed.*

**140 (below)    Harveys of Bristol, 1939**
*The original bottling area in the Denmark Street cellars, is now the
site of Harveys Restaurant. On 24 November 1940 Harveys'
headquarters in Denmark Street was destroyed by a bomb.
Miraculously, the 13th-century cellars, with their stock of vintage
wines, survived the bombing.*

**141 (right)    Castle Street, c.1913**
*Castle Street was built upon the inner ward of the castle following
its demolition in 1655. By the 1870s many of the 17th- and
18th-century buildings had been replaced and it had already become
Bristol's most popular shopping area.*

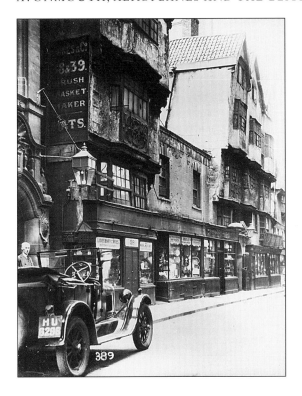

*142 (above left)*   **Wine Street in the 1920s**
*Since a pillory once stood at this junction, and a 'wynch' was on the pillory, Wine Street could be a corruption of Wynch Street. On the right-hand side is the Dutch house and High Street. Hidden from us on the same side were Jones' stores, The Don, and Baker Baker. Most of the big stores had premises here.*

*143 (left)   **Castle Street in the 1930s***
*During the 1930s many of the older shops were replaced by a series of chain stores. This was certainly the busiest of Bristol's shopping streets but was blitzed on 24 November 1940. The shopping area was rebuilt as Broadmead.*

*144 (above)   **Mary-le-Port Street, 1920s***
*On the extreme left is the entrance to the church. Numbers 39 and 38 next to it are J. Jones and Co. City Brush Works, which made baskets and brushes and sold ladies' boots and shoes. Above the boot shop is a carving of Arms of Guilds. Further down the street are typical 16th-century buildings.*

*145 (above right)   **The Nails outside the Corn Exchange, 1930s***
*Four brass 'Nails' outside the Corn Exchange were used by merchants in lieu of tables for making payments or writing, hence 'to pay on the nail'. Three of the Nails came from the Tolsey alongside All Saints' Church, another came from outside the old Council House. In the 1670s there were six of them.*

Corsham to avoid the possibility of the industry being destroyed by bombing. The Blenheim was succeeded by the Beaufort and by the Beaufighter. 2,753 aircraft were built in Bristol itself, and 100,032 Bristol engines were produced, representing 38.5 per cent of the country's total war output, excluding jet engines.

The activity of the port, which at its peak in 1945 was 5,782,000 tons of shipping entering Avonmouth, together with the several aircraft factories, inevitably made the city a target for bombing. Raids occurred in 1940, 1941, and a few in 1942. 1,299 people were killed by bombs, yet the city's main industrial areas escaped major damage. The ancient heart of the city, St Peter's Street, Mary-le-Port, the Dutch House, St Peter's Hospital, Castle Street, The Horsefair, Stokes Croft, part of St James' Square, Temple Church and the Merchants' Hall, were destroyed. Part of the Merchants' Almshouses, part of the Llandoger Trow, the University's Great

**146   Bristol Bridge, 1923**
*Traffic congestion by 1860 necessitated widening Bridges' 1768
structure. Iron cantilevers supported footpaths on either side. That on
the western side was completed in 1873-4. The photograph is looking
up High Street towards Christchurch.*

Hall, sections of Park Street, and the nave of St
Nicholas and the area round Temple Meads were
damaged badly. By good fortune, St Mary Redcliffe,
and the Lord Mayor's Chapel, St James' and the
cathedral, the Red Lodge and Wesley's Chapel were
all spared.

Apart from the growth of Avonmouth, and the
expansion of the aircraft industry, there were
significant developments in education. Bristol
acquired two universities. The vision and drive of
John Percival, Headmaster of Clifton College, John
Addington Symonds, Benjamin Jowett of Balliol,
Catherine Winkworth, Lewis Fry, and Bishop

Frederick Temple of Exeter, led to the calling of a
meeting in the Victoria Rooms, in 1874, to promote
a College of Science and Literature. The College
opened in 1876 in two houses in Park Row with 87
day students and 234 in evening classes. The Medical
School became part of this reorganised University
College in 1893. It was the first University College
to admit women. The Fry and the Wills families

**147    Bedminster Tram Depot, 4 January 1941**
*At 6a.m. on 4 January a large bomb destroyed the approach tracks and damaged most of the rolling stock. A driver about to drive out one of the trams was killed. Numbers 236, 87 and 136 took most of the blast. This was the city's fourth severe night raid, known as the 'Freeze Blitz'. Water froze the firemen's hoses that night.*

**148    The Dutch House, 25 November 1940**
*It appears the bomb fell at 10.20p.m. on 24 November. The Dutch House was pulled down by soldiers two days later. From the photograph it is difficult to see how it could have been restored, although some have claimed that only the top two floors were damaged.*

**149    A frozen fire ladder, 4 January 1941**
*This famous photograph of the Bristol Blitz indicates one of the problems faced by firefighters in the winter of 1941. The Fire Brigade was 77 men understrength. Some fires needed five to ten pumping appliances each. There were 224 pump appliances available.*

**150    Park Street, 24 November 1940**
*Bristol had suffered 1,159 deaths from enemy action up to this time, fewer than Birmingham or Liverpool, but still the sixth highest number in the country. On 24 November 30 shops in Park Street were totally destroyed and a further six burnt out. Three more were seriously damaged.*

made several large monetary gifts in the following years. Besides the University College there had existed since 1885 an institution known as the Merchants' Technical School, later College, which taught engineering. New buildings for the University College sprung up in University Road between 1879 and 1905, and in 1908 Henry Overton Wills announced that he would give what was then the immense sum of £100,000 if a Chartered University were created by amalgamating University College with the Merchants' Technical College. The Charter of Bristol's first university was granted by the crown

*151 (left)   Horsefair, 1954*
*Excavations are in progress prior to rebuilding John Lewis and the rest of Broadmead. In an attack lasting 4½ hours, starting at 6.30p.m., 12,500 bombs were dropped by 135 aircraft for the loss of two planes on 24 November 1940. Two hundred lives were lost and 689 people were injured. Much of the central area of the city was destroyed.*

*152 (below left)   Castle Street, c.1954*
*The devastation wrought by bombing on the night of 24 November is still apparent, especially when this photograph is compared with that taken in the 1930s. There is no Boots, no Marks and Spencer, no Woolworths, no Jones, and no Brooks. At least the rubble has gone.*

*153 (below)   Broadmead, 13 January 1954*
*Bomb damage sites are still open plots. On the extreme right is Marks and Spencer. Scaffolding enfolds all three adjacent sites. The Clock Shop, established in 1887, survived the Blitz at its site at the junction of Milk Street with Old King Street, but the shop was demolished in 1954.*

on 21 May 1909, and Henry Overton Wills became the first Chancellor. The whole dynasty of the Wills family made generous donations of millions of pounds over many years for the city's benefit, restoring St Mary Redcliffe, improving the cathedral, building and endowing St Monica's Home of Rest (1920), creating the University Buildings at the top of Park Street, the Royal Fort Physics Laboratory, purchasing Clifton Hill House as a Hall of Residence, and the Victoria Rooms as a Students' Union building. Between 1925 and 1929 the collegiate Hall of Residence for men arose on an estate purchased for the University on the Downs by Sir George Alfred Wills in memory of his brother.

In making these significant contributions to the city's social and cultural activities, the Wills family helped confirm Bristol's position as the unofficial

regional capital of the south-west. In the latter part of the 20th century a second university emerged called the University of the West of England (UWE), with a campus at Frenchay, which quickly established an enviable reputation for research and teaching excellence. Emerging as a polytechnic in 1969 from a merger of local Colleges of Commerce and of Arts and Design, it was soon enlarged by amalgamating with the Colleges of Education at St Matthias and at Redland in 1976. It was given independence from Avon in April 1989 as a Higher Education Corporation, and achieved University status in October 1992 with its own degrees.

As Bristol increasingly became the 'metropolis of the West', the demand for goods and services stimulated the growth of commerce and industry in the area. In June 1960 the aircraft side of the Bristol Aeroplane Company amalgamated with Vickers and English Electric to form the Bristol Aircraft Corporation. Similarly, in 1966, the engine department which had previously merged with Armstrong Siddeley, was absorbed by Rolls Royce. These developments ensured that aircraft and engine production continued at Filton, and that it remained the south west of England's largest industrial employer.

*154 (top)   **Clifton College (architect, Charles F. Hanson)***
*The chapel with its detached spire was completed in 1866, and various buildings in the Gothic style were added up to the 1920s. The school served as General Omar Bradley's headquarters during the Second World War. Earl Kitchener looks out over the cricket field where so many of his officers once played.*

*155 (far left)   **Wills Memorial Building, c.1920***
*The most striking feature of the Bristol skyline was designed by Sir George Oatley in 1911, but progress was delayed by the First World War and it was not completed until 1925. The tower houses a 9½-ton bell, Great George, which was then the fourth largest bell in England.*

*156 (left)   **University Great Hall, 25 November 1940***
*The raid of 24 November destroyed the Great Hall and its glorious hammerbeam roof, one of the finest in England. It was being used as the library for King's College, London, and contained many thousands of books brought down for their students. The Wills family immediately set aside seasoned oak to rebuild the hall after the war.*

In this short survey of Bristol Past one can only point to the way that, since the Second World War, Bristol has seen an influx of Banking (Lloyds), Insurance (Sun Life), and other institutions escaping from London's high property rents. New jobs in the service sector have strengthened Bristol's traditional role as the administrative and distribution centre for the west of England, alongside a continued commitment to light industry. The construction of the Ministry of Defence's centralised Procurement Establishment in the area has strengthened this trend. Perhaps more than most other urban communities, Bristol has shown the spirit of the Merchant Venturers to compete and survive.

One such Merchant Venturer founded in 1634 England's oldest girls' school, the 'Red Maids'. Their school arms are those of the Spanish Company to which Whitson belonged. The founding of Cheltenham College, Marlborough, Radley, Oundle and Wellington in the 19th century was followed by the opening of Bristol's own comparable public school, at Clifton, in 1862. Bristol Grammar School, founded by Robert and Nicholas Thorne in St Bartholomew's Hospital, might have been among the wealthiest schools in England if the founders' original intentions had been carried out. St Bartholomew's lands as well as the buildings were to have been made over to the school by Nicholas' will in 1546, when the Corporation became the governors. The lands which lay north of the town and are now covered by Bristol's suburbia, however, were otherwise used by Nicholas Thorne II, and then his daughter Alice Pykes. Most were sold and did not reach the school. After a Chancery case some of the lands were recovered in 1617.

A soapboiler, John Carr, in 1586 left lands and revenues for Queen Elizabeth's Hospital School, modelled on Christ's Hospital. The school began in the Master's Lodge of St Mark's Hospital (Gaunts). The Cathedral School, replacing an Abbey Choir school, was refounded when St Augustine's became a

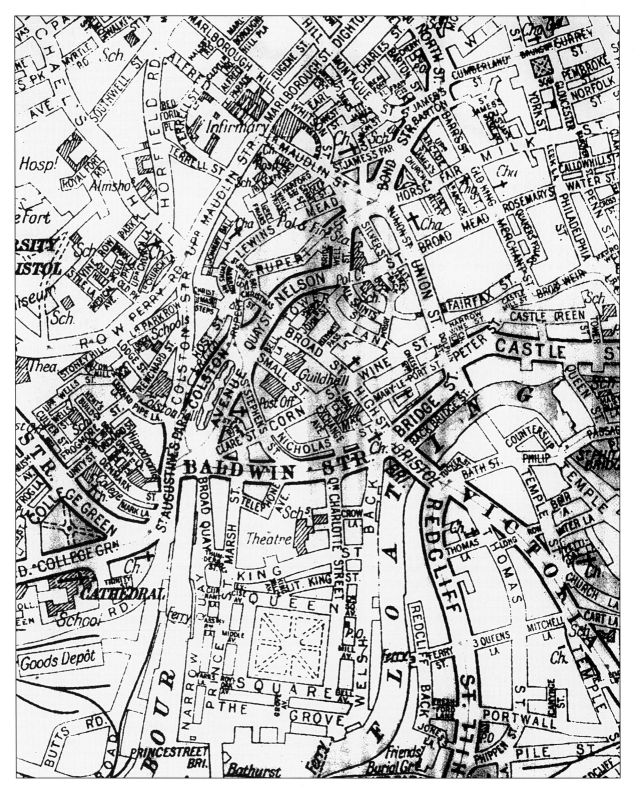

*157 (opposite)* **Bristol before the war, the 1937 map**
*This section of the central area shows Bristol before the covering in of the Frome, before the bisection of Queen Square, and before Barr Street and Old King Street disappeared in the rebuilt Broadmead.*

*158 (above)*
**Royal Fort House and the Queen's Building, 1960**
*The most prominent hill in Bristol was capped in 1929 with the Harry Wills Physics Laboratory, designed by Sir George Oatley. Harry Wills had bought the Tyndall estate and gave it to the University. The Queen's Building, which encircles the hill, housed Mathematics, Engineering and Geology when it was opened by Queen Elizabeth on 5 December 1958.*

cathedral in 1542. Clifton High school for Girls was founded in 1877 before John Percival had moved on from being Headmaster of Clifton, and he was Vice-President of the High School's Council. In the school's cricket team were two daughters of W.G. Grace. Redland High School was founded in 1882, with John Percival as President of its Council. These schools took good care of the children of Bristol's middle class, though from 1709 to 1838 QEH could only

afford to pay its masters for one year contracts, and had become a charity boarding school with admission by nomination. It moved to its Brandon Hill site in 1847 and admission by examination began in 1875. Together with Colston's High Anglican foundation (1710), which moved to its Stapleton site in 1861, and Colston Girls (1891), St Brendan's RC School for 600 boys, and La Retraite (1924) for 360 RC girls, there were also a number of grammar schools set up by the school boards as Higher Grade Schools. St George opened to serve Bristol's Gloucester suburb in 1894 with 500 children. Merrywood opened in 1906 to serve south Bristol. Fairfield opened in 1898 with 600 pupils. There was also Rose Green High School (1952) and Cotham Grammar School, originally a responsibility of the Merchant Venturers. Since the mid-20th century efforts have been made to provide an equally good education for all Bristol's children.

After the Butler Education Act Education Committees had to assume responsibility for secondary schooling for all children. Twenty-two schools with 8,000 places were destroyed by bombing in the war. These had to be replaced quickly and to be open to all children in neighbourhoods such as Henbury, Lockleaze, Hengrove, Monks Park, Pen Park, Greenway, Bishopston, Bedminster Down and Portway. While the existence in the city of a large number of Independent and Public Schools is a commentary on the educational enterprise and charitable vision of Bristolians hitherto, equality of opportunity is now recognised as a desirable goal. Bristol's newer schools have had an uphill struggle against existing status, tradition, selection, and the willingness and ability to pay.

Bristol still has the oldest theatre remaining in this country, founded in 1766. It launched the first provincial newspaper in 1702, and the first provincial partnership bank, known as the 'Old Bank'. In Queen Square, Bristol had the first American Consulate in England. The Public Library in King Street, started in 1613 by Robert Redwood, was the first in the provinces, after Norwich. From Bristol John Wesley launched the greatest single religious initiative since the Reformation, and from the same city Mary Carpenter and Hannah More sought to foster a humanitarian commitment which spread far outside the city's boundaries. Centred at the meeting of the M4 and M5 with two magnificent bridges across to Wales, with an exceedingly profitable port at Avonmouth, and good rail communication to London and to the continent, Bristol has grounds for optimism that its future will be at least as colourful and significant as its past.

**159   Second Severn Crossing, January 2000**
*Commencing in 1992 and finishing, on time, in 1996, Laing, GTM-Entrepose constructed a cable-stayed bridge 948 metres long. It is approached by viaducts on the Avon side 2,103 metres long and on the Gwent side, 2,077 metres long.*

# Further Reading

## I  Brigg-Stow, the Place of the Bridge

Branigan, K., *The Romans In the Bristol Area*, Brist. Hist. Assoc., no. 22 (1969)

Grinsell, L.V., *The Bristol Mint*, Brist. Hist. Assoc., no. 30 (1972)

Savage, Anne (ed.), *The Anglo/Saxon Chronicles* (Godalming, 1995)

## II  Wine, Woad and Guilds

Bickley, Francis (ed.), *The Little Red Book of Bristol*, 2 vols. (Bristol and London, 1900)

Crawford, Anne, *Bristol and the Wine Trade*, Brist. Hist. Assoc., no. 57 (1984)

Jones, R.H., *Excavations in Redcliffe, 1983-85*, City of Bristol Museum and Art Gallery (1986)

Price, Roger, *Excavations at St Bartholomews Hospital, Bristol*, City of Bristol Museum and Art Gallery (1979)

Ralph, Elizabeth (ed.), *The Great White Book*, Bristol Record Soc., XXXII (1979)

Sherborne, James, *The Port of Bristol in the Middle Ages*, Brist. Hist. Assoc., no. 13 (1965)

## III  Voyages and Venturers

Fleming, Peter and Costello, Kieron, *Discovering Cabot's Bristol* (Bristol, 1998)

Jones, Donald, *Captain Woodes Rogers' Voyage Round the World 1708-11*, Brist. Hist. Assoc., no.79 (1992)

Quinn, David, *Sebastian Cabot and Bristol Exploration*, Brist. Hist. Assoc., no. 21 (1968, revised 1993)

Vanes, Jean, *The Port of Bristol in the 16th century*, Brist. Hist. Assoc., no. 39 (1977)

Wilson, E.M. Carus, *The Merchant Adventurers of Bristol in the 15th century*, Brist. Hist. Assoc., no. 4 (1962)

## IV  Reformation, Civil War and Servants to Plantations

Baskerville, G., 'The Dispossessed Religious of Gloucestershire', *Trans. of the B. and G. Arch. Soc.*, Vol. XLIX (1927), pp.63-122.

Bettey, Joseph, *The Suppression of the Religious Houses in Bristol*, Brist. Hist. Assoc., no.74 (1990)

Lynch, John, *For King and Parliament, Bristol and the Civil War* (Sutton, 1999)

McGrath, Patrick, *Bristol and the Civil War*, Brist. Hist. Assoc., no. 50 (1981)

Souden, David, 'Rogues, whores and vagabonds? Indentured servant emigrants to North America, and the case of mid-17th-century Bristol', *Social History*, III, 1978, pp.499-540.

## V  Slaves, Sugar and Tobacco

Jones, Donald, *Bristol's Sugar Trade and Refining Industry*, Brist. Hist. Assoc., no. 89 (1996)

McGrath, Patrick, 'Merchant Venturers and Bristol Shipping in the early 17th century', *Mariner's Mirror*, Vol. 36, no. 1, pp.69-80.

Morgan, Kenneth, 'Bristol West India Merchants in the 18th century', *Trans. of the Royal Hist. Assoc.*, 6th series, Vol. III (1993), pp.185-208.

Richardson, David, *The Bristol Slave Traders; A Collective Portrait*, Brist. Hist. Assoc., no. 60 (1985)

## VI    Georgian Bristol: Merchants and Methodists

Jones, Donald, *A History of Clifton* (Phillimore, 1992)

Morgan, Kenneth, *John Wesley in Bristol*, Brist. Hist. Assoc., no. 75 (1990)

Morgan, Kenneth, *Edward Colston and Bristol*, Brist. Hist. Assoc., no. 96 (1999)

Press, Jonathan, *The Merchant Seamen of Bristol, 1747-1789*, Brist. Hist. Assoc., no. 38 (1976, reprinted 1995)

Underdown, P.T., *Bristol and Burke*, Brist. Hist. Assoc., no. 2, (1961)

## VII    Brunel's Bristol and Popular Discontents

Buchanan, R. Angus, 'Brunel in Bristol' in Patrick McGrath and John Cannon (eds.), *Essays in Bristol and Gloucester History* (Bristol, 1976)

Manson, Michael, *'Riot', The Bristol Bridge Massacre of 1793* (Bristol, 1997)

Rolt, L.T.C., *Isambard Kingdom Brunel* (London, 1957)

Thomas, Susan, *The Bristol Riots*, Brist. Hist. Assoc., no. 34 (1974)

## VIII    Shipbuilding, Sugar, Coal and Public Health

Alford, B.W.E., 'The economic development of Bristol in the 19th century; an enigma?', in McGrath and Cannon (eds.), *Essays in Bristol and Gloucester History* (Bristol, 1976)

Dresser, Madge and Ollerenshaw, Philip (eds.), *The Making of Modern Bristol* (Bristol, 1996)

Charles Harvey and John Press, 'Industrial Change and the economic life of Bristol since 1800', in Charles Harvey and Jon Press (eds.), *Studies in the Business History of Bristol* (Bristol, 1988)

Large, David and Round, Frances, *Public Health in mid-Victorian Bristol*, Brist. Hist. Assoc., no. 35 (1974)

Ralph, Elizabeth and Cobb, Peter, *New Anglican Churches in 19th Century Bristol*, Brist. Hist. Assoc., no. 76 (1991)

## IX    Avonmouth, Aeroplances and the Blitz

Harvey, Charles and Press, Jon, *Sir George White of Bristol, 1854-1916*, Brist. Hist. Assoc., no. 72 (1989)

Penny, John, *Luftwaffe Operations over Bristol, 1940/44*, Brist. Branch of Hist. Assoc., no. 85 (1995)

Stone, Glyn, 'Rearmament, War and the performance of the Bristol Aeroplane Company, 1935-45' in Harvey and Press (eds.), *Studies in the Business History of Bristol* (Bristol, 1988)

# Index

Page numbers in **bold** denote illustrations. C – century.

*Lavar's panoramic view from a balloon, 1887.* Queen Square and St Augustine's Reach are to the left. Temple Meads is to the right.